10X Your Business in 2019

Learn How the Most Successful Entrepreneurs are Paying their Way to the Top and Scaling their Personal Brands with Social Media Marketing on Facebook, YouTube & Instagram

Written by Joel Johnsson

purposes only. All effort has been executed to present accurate, up to date, and reliable, complete information. No warranties of any kind are declared or implied. Readers acknowledge that the author is not engaging in the rendering of legal, financial, medical or professional advice. The content within this book has been derived from various sources. Please consult a licensed professional before attempting any techniques outlined in this book.

By reading this document, the reader agrees that under no circumstances is the author responsible for any losses, direct or indirect, which are incurred as a result of the use of information contained within this document, including, but not limited to, — errors, omissions, or inaccuracies.

Table of Contents

Introduction

Thank you for choosing this eBook to learn about the latest social media marketing tips and tricks. The chapters will focus on the significance of social media marketing and the way it has influenced modern day business strategies. It will also give you an insight into how the top players of the contemporary online industry implement it into their businesses.

Social media marketing is using the online network and various platforms of social media to sell and promote its services and products. It includes far more than what it used to, as so many new platforms have risen to provide users with modes of entertainment. So, to run a successful business online, one needs to use all available sources – including social media platforms. These include gaining traffic through various methods and running advertisements on Facebook, Google, Instagram, YouTube, etc.

A section of this business marketing plan can

focus on gathering followings on YouTube or Instagram, but that should not be your objective in 2019. Your main goal should be to Make Money. To achieve that, you will have to sell your services and products. You simply do not make money by accumulating lots of followers on your social media account. With tons of followers, you are just generating tons of leads, which can later turn into potential customers when you provide them with interesting products and services.

Thus, using a large following is just the first step toward a prolonged online moneymaking business plan. You need to understand what has influenced the year 2019. Social media, nowadays, has changed a lot since the previous years.

As an example, YouTube channels had significant organic growth in the year 2017, which has enabled many unknown or aspiring channels to gather huge followings by the end of 2018. Their main technique to achieve this had been by posting videos consistently. Out of the blue, one or two of their videos would go viral, leading to their overnight success on the web. Their exposure and increasing subscriber count would help them achieve their business goals later. Similar experiences have been seen on other social media marketing platforms.

So, you should know that organic growth was much easier in previous years. However, things have changed now. You cannot follow the same grinding tactic anymore. You will have to religiously understand the exposure techniques and methods used in the year 2019, and that too inexpensively. Mind that Instagram, Facebook, YouTube, etc., are all social media businesses with similar goals, which is to make money.

Thus, to earn more, you will need ads on your accounts in 2019. You can consider it a smarter way to achieve growth online. There is limited time for grinding for 10 years or so. You need to have a following or subscribers, no doubt – but you are also going to require additional sense to implement online business tactics for 2019 on your social media platforms. This is possible when you have services and products for your following.

So, it is time to dig into this world and understand how things work for you in 2019.

Knowing Social Media in 2019

Note that social media is consistently affecting people's everyday lives in the contemporary world. You can witness almost everyone using it daily.

If you have a business in the present world, and if you have already been neglecting the world of social media, now is your time to do it. Consider it to be a significant addition to your business, and it is a brilliant approach to get in more customers. Furthermore, it is almost free of cost!

Here are some vital information for you to grasp:

Over 3 billion people are currently using social media accounts in today's world, which is a 13% hike from the year 2018. Most people out of these, use their social media account at least once a month. Just America on average uses social media accounts for 2 hours or more every day.

With most people active on social media, your business needs to be an active portal there too. 75% of the top online marketers state that an increase in efforts involving social media marketing helped them grow traffic for their business significantly. Plus, they found an increase in 50% sales due to their efforts online. One-third of the users associated with social media accounts use their accounts for finding information related to products or services.

Making your personal brand using social media in today's world is especially vital. You will have to assure yourself that you have worked on a great and successful brand that truly interacts with the customers. For that, this book will help you in understanding how you can achieve it in 2019.

Once again, by choosing this book, you have

made the right choice, as you are about to learn the right way of implementing social media marketing tactics for 2019.

Chapter 1: Why Social Media Is Significant In Creating an Online Business?

To help you understand it in simple terms: our business requires an online platform, and just having a website is not enough to promote or establish your business on the Internet.

The niche or genre of your business is of little importance here. You can own a small store that has just a hundred customers a week or you could be the owner of a multimillion-dollar franchise of restaurants, you will have to have an online presence on social media platforms. You may be a freelance model who signs contracts worth thousands of dollars for endorsing products for customers, or you could be the owner of a saloon. Everyone, who owns a business and is finding methods to earn more money has to have a platform on social media.

It is an important section of any strategy involving online business. If you have not created your social media accounts until now, then it is high time for it. While many people in the world still do not use social media sites, the number is still smaller compared to the ones who use it on a daily basis. Moreover, such people, who had been inactive in the past, are also learning to be a part of such platforms so that they can connect with others in this vast digital world.

In the past ten years, the structure of the online world has had a drastic change. Most of this has been an influence from social media. Eventually, it has ended up becoming one of the main tools for businesses and brands. Thus, it is crucial for you to join this network to increase your authority in the public and engage with potential customers for increasing your sales.

Do have this thought in your brain: businesses still can function pretty well without implementing social media. They can earn profits, or even end up bankrupt. However, for consistent growth of your business, if you want to keep making money and enhance the product/services sales results constantly, if you want to develop a fruitful relationship with the consumers and interact with them without the need of spending extra on your promotion tactics, social media is an essential factor.

Another thing to keep in mind is that, as the number of people involving in social media increase, the number of people searching for brands and businesses of interest will also increase. Such people are looking forward to interacting with you regarding your products and services. Deep inside, they want you to care for them through your services and products. If you connect with your customers and fulfill their requirements properly, you can increase your profits. This will be possible when you have a connection with them throughout your business relationship.

Building up your profile through social media marketing is not as easy as it seems, especially when it involves business. You can consider it to be a vital project that involves the use of a plethora of tactics, platforms, and engagements. Due to the level of challenge one faces while setting it up for their businesses, many back out and think that social media is not meant for them.

However, it is meant for them. It is completely worth the struggle.

The following reasons will help you understand the importance of social media marketing.

For Building Awareness

You can consider social media to be a part of your everyday life. You can witness people using social media to talk about themselves, their lives. Their updates on such platforms cover up what they eat, where they work, where they are having their vacation, what they are wearing, who they are dating, where do they like to travel, what they like, where they live, etc. You can find it all online. Sometimes, you just think that you know a person too well just through such updates.

When an individual posts something on social

media, all of his or her closest friends or followers in his or her list learn about it. If some of those closest friends tend to share the post, then all the closest friends of those individuals learn about it. This number keeps growing, making the post visible to folks who had nothing to do with the first person, who created the post initially. And, this chain keeps on going. People keep on sharing such posts, and more and more people come to know about it. The same can happen if you, as a company, create an interesting post for your followers.

An average consumer converses about brands with friends, colleagues, and family members at least 90 times weekly. In fact, at least 50% of the individuals who tend to buy something actually end up buying just because of a recommendation in their social media account for a service or product.

Understand that: half of the population active on social media has bought something because of social media posts and promotions. With active participation on social media, you are luring more customers to your business page, to your firm, to your services/products, and ultimately to more sales.

Moreover, you are not limited to local listings of your products and services on social media. This platform offers you the opportunity to spread awareness around the world. Bringing your products and services for international customers is your choice though. For example: you are owning a gym and are into health and fitness. A simple Instagram account involving your daily posts can have a great impact on the people following you from anywhere around the world. If you have a restaurant that has a special dish available only at your place, then tweeting about it online can indulge many users to try that dish at your restaurant.

For Controlling Image

By using your own name online with your business, you can regulate what the people hear and see about you. Understand it like this:

When you google "KFC," what results show up on your screen? You will see their website, a number of KFC restaurants in your area, etc. However, the most important thing you will notice is a list of all social media pages linked to KFC, more particularly their Facebook and Twitter pages. If KFC did not have an online presence, what do you think would end up in the search results?

You may end up seeing a couple of articles dissing the restaurant's food, some negative comments and posts involving unsatisfied customers, or perhaps a couple of positive feedbacks too. Surely, typing "KFC" in your google search page does not show up these results, as KFC owns social media pages and a website, which regulates their image on the first page of Google. The firm controls what a user, who was searching for them, sees first on the page.

You can also test it out too. If you own a Facebook page, especially when you try searching for the name of your registered business, you will see it at the top of the google search result. Most probably, a customer who is searching for you will click on that first result involving your business. Thus, you have the power to control your image and everything that people will see about you through your social media accounts.

For Showing Authenticity

People have an urge to learn what is behind the walls of a business. They want to learn more about your image, your work, etc. They want to have the feeling that they know who you are. With social media, you have the ability to cultivate your personal brand, and eventually create a feeling that your brand has real people present in it.

You may have seen a number of ads where companies show their employees working. This tactic is used to display a sense of realism when involving the promotion of a business. When you tend to understand that business is not about money, but people, the method of attracting customers automatically opens for you. When you focus on the people, you no longer represent yourself as a corporation that is just there to make profits. You tend to show that you have people employed under you. You show individuals that you put efforts in making brilliant services and products for them by taking care of the community. As a result, you end up becoming authentic, and people start trusting you and your business.

For Encouraging Engagement

Engagement involves interacting with people on social media, with the help of shares, likes, and comments. This is crucial on social media for keeping in touch with your potential customers.

A good example of a company that has been great at communicating with its customers is Lush. If you are not aware of their presence yet, they manufacture beauty products like hair and face masks, etc. You have to acknowledge the brilliance of their social media marketing team. If you type the world Lush with a hashtag in the search bar on almost any social media webpage, you will end up seeing tons of videos related to them.

Lush has used its social media marketing team to share videos with everyday individuals using bath bomb explosions in water, after effects of beauty products on hair and skin, and pictures of people using facemasks. This is active because the company asks of its followers to share their pictures and videos with people using their products in various ways. Plus, they encourage them to use the relevant hashtags too. This simple, yet fun technique ends up promoting their business and increases their brand awareness online.

It further makes their audience feel connected with them, as they feel special when involving in creating videos and photos for the company. So, by offering your audience the opportunity to be close to your company, and involving them in such fun activities, you encourage them to know more about who you and your company are. You are lifting that curtain between you and your audience and increasing transparency. That way, people will feel trust your services and products more often, and eventually end up buying them.

For Providing Support

Anyone who has experienced the hardships related to customer services knows the exhaustion and frustration. It becomes even more irritating when the issue involved could have been easily solved if the information related to it was offered to you in an easy and quick fashion.

Surely, this issue can be fixed using a simple inquiry section on a social media page, like Facebook or website. You can also answer the questions put up by your customers in the comment section of posts you have shared, or even message them directly. Social media accounts have so many advantages of such types, which do not involve the cumbersome calling off each and every customer and irritating them for no reason. Do note that, solving a problem for a customer as quickly as possible will maintain your image and brand reputation high.

For Knowing Your Target Audience

Note that the individuals who will tend to follow you on social media accounts will mostly comprise of people who really have an interest in your company, services and products. Such individuals will believe in what you have to say, and will be actively wanting or using your products and services. This can be beneficial in a way. You will have the advantage of knowing the person whom you are going to sell your products and services.

Also, you will have the right information related to your followers. Several social media websites, like Instagram and Twitter, have brilliant tools like polling for your followers. You can provide your followers with multiple products or services using it and learn about what your customers are exactly interested in.

You Have An Influence Over Them

Using social media, you have the power of

posting an unlimited number of times every day. While there is no limit to the frequency of your posts, do keep in mind that posting over 100 times every day might be too much. Your posts should involve a specific schedule that can help engage your audience in interacting with your business. By constantly updating posts and communicating with your audience, you are building a place in their minds at all times.

If you are into the clothing business, and an individual who follows you is looking to buy some apparel, the chances are that he or she might end up visiting your online shopping portal to buy the clothing from you. When he or she logs into his or her Facebook account, and sees that you have promoted a new collection of apparel for your customers, it becomes very likely that the person will approach you to buy the product.

By nailing the opportunity every time to assure your audience of your presence and business online, your followers will start connecting with you automatically and buy products or services that you offer more frequently. Just imagine the times you have visited a coffee shop just because of the advertisement you saw online related to it. Would that image in your mind, due to the advertisement, not indulge you to try out that coffee whenever you have a craving for it? You surely will!

It Is Cheap

For any single problem, a conflict involving a business, economics is the basic factor. Any person involving in buying something will always have the question in mind: can I afford it? You can find this factor associated with any business, where high profits are always the most crucial aspect related to any business. It also enlightens one to understand how their business will handle itself in the competitive online world.

Campaigns related to marketing in business are quite common. Most major firms have at least one individual involved in the advertisement campaigns. However, such campaigns can also involve huge investments, which can accumulate to a lot of expenses at times. For large companies, such a budget is planned. But, for small businesses, this amount is often a luxury.

With social media, that investment in advertising is diminished. Plus, it is even better than most marketing campaigns. It is quite affordable and does not even require much of your time. Surely, time is money, and this marketing strategy has the best influence compared to all other tactics.

If you study the right approach to implement social media for your business, you can end up gaining the same results, or even better, as you would have done with a marketing campaign involving thousands of dollars.

It Is Easy To Learn

You may feel that social media platform is quite daunting, especially if you are someone who is new to all this experience. Fortunately, it is not as difficult as it seems. It may feel like an intricate activity, and you may think that it will involve weeks or months of training beforehand. But, it is quite simple actually. All you have to do is spend a small amount of time and have patience while going through the various social media accounts you want to associate with. Plus, help from this book will also be beneficial for you to survive in the social marketing world in 2019 and beyond.

In the contemporary world, most people use social media on their smart devices, which you can also indulge into. You can update your posts, read feeds, and whatnot through your phone. You can also access multiple account feeds through apps nowadays that have all simplified the way users interact with each other online.

Most importantly, social media platform for marketing is here for a long time. It will stay for as long as you are alive, which is why it is high time that you use it for your business as much as possible. The faster you learn it, the better benefits you can extract out of it for your business. Your media strategy will represent your business and help it gain more followers and potential customers in the end.

To start, you will first need to understand which social media sites are best for your business. Surely, you may want to approach building your reputation and presence using the most popular social media platform. But, understand that it is not a prudent idea. If this is your first time, then you should not involve in this strategy as it can be a huge error. All this strategy will do is take you straight into a situation where you feel overwhelmed and inadequate. It can also have a negative impact on your business.

No doubt, it feels like joining the most popular social media site for starting with the branding strategy feels logical, but it does not always work for all types of businesses. In fact, every social media platform has its own targeted demographic. You may not be able to locate the right customers if you have set up your social media pages on the wrong platform.

Furthermore, it is not a prudent idea to involve in all social media sites present to start your online business-marketing journey. Did you start running instantly when you were a baby? No, you started crawling first, and then learned to walk, and later, run. You should not feel ashamed if you are new to social media. A prudent, simple, and logical step to enter into the world of social media marketing is by understanding what your objective from it is. Then, you will be able to find the perfect match for your marketing campaign.

You can use the following information to help you get started with the right social media platform. You can find the most popular social media sites available for business marketing nowadays. The following platforms are also listed based on their popularity numbers. You will find information related to how they operate and whether they will be a prudent choice for you or not.

Facebook: This platform sits on the throne of the social media platforms list. It was introduced at a time when social media was beginning to shape up. Facebook was lucky enough to quickly gain popularity due to new and better ways of communicating with other users. Facebook presently has 2.27 billion users actively using it, which is almost 1/3 of the popular of the world. It is also the social media platform, which you cannot skip, if you are involved in setting up an online marketing campaign for your business. It is a simple platform that involves adapting itself as per the feedback, experience, and needs of the users.

Based on the type of business one is involved in, most individuals can find a way of marketing on Facebook. You can find over 66 million pages involving some sort of business on Facebook at present. And, most of these pages are there as they are easy to handle, with several features to utilize. Moreover, every format of content can easily match with the platform of Facebook, which includes stories, videos, photos, text, etc. You can also use the benefit of Facebook's messenger application to advertise your service or product to the followers added in your created page groups. Thus, Facebook can be considered to be a vital platform for most businesses. Currently, almost 80% of millennials are active on Facebook, but teenagers are shifting from that platform to involve in other social media sites, which this book will discuss later.

YouTube: This video-sharing site is a place where you can find entertainment for hours. You can indulge yourself in cat videos, cooking videos, gameplay, etc. without running out of content. YouTube comprises of over 2 billion active users and that number has since been increasing. Furthermore, it is also considered to be the second biggest search engine present online, right after Google (which also owns it). All you need to do on YouTube is to set up a channel and upload original videos that you have created. People who will like your videos will subscribe to your channel, comment on it, like it and share it with others. That way, you can gain popularity eventually.

The platform of YouTube is great for influential executives, who talk about experiences with different companies and people, and review products. Furthermore, they are also for bloopers or behind the scene montage and how-to videos. If you are interested in cookware, then you could upload tutorial videos on how to use pans and pots properly. If you're involved in selling vegetables, then you can increase your following by showing them how to grow vegetables. You can even create Q and A videos where you answer queries offered by your audience. Video content can have a great influence when you implement it using social media. However, note that it will involve more effort than just creating an account on other platforms like Facebook. If you feel that it is worth it, then you can use it.

Instagram: Here is another popular app that has garnered an impressive following of over 400 million users active. This platform has been popular among the younger generation, who love to post updates related to lifestyle, art, travel, fashion, and food. It also has other features, most of which are mostly simple to use, including live videos and stories. Furthermore, Instagram has lately launched another platform by the name IGTV that is the same as YouTube, which is meant for videos or longer duration.

There is still time to see if IGTV would be worth the risk or not. Nevertheless, Instagram is a great photo-sharing site and application. If you are involved in a brand that is visually appealing, such as a model or an artist, then Instagram can be your way to increase in followers and sales. You can also consider it a feasible platform for the ones who love to blog about food, fashion, and travel. However, do note that it is mostly favored as a mobile app, which is why it will have limited use on a desktop.

Twitter: This social media platform is great for sharing feeds and updates. After all, it has over 330 million users active. Twitter implements its unique selling point in real-time marketing tactics. It gives you updates about what is happening in the present time related to entertainment, politics, sports, and news.

Furthermore, you are allowed to use a maximum of 280 characters for each post. This can be challenging for some to promote their services and products or share some news. However, the ones who can use this platform skillfully have gained great benefits. Moreover, people tend to respond better to posts that are short, as they take little time to read. Eventually, there is a higher chance of such posts to be shared as well.

In fact, Twitter was the actual catalyst for triggering the potential of customer service through the implementation of social media. Companies and celebrities initiated utilizing Twitter as a mode of direct communication with their followers and fans. Ultimately, fans too felt that they could connect directly to their favorite celebrities and companies on this platform. So, they went there.

At present, at least 80% of customer services involving social media have implemented Twitter to solve queries. Some people will still find it hard to accept the use of just 280 characters.

Plus, there is also the involvement of constant posting of tweets to keep the followers involved. This can be tiring for some. However, most find Twitter pretty useful, so it is here to work for you.

Snapchat: Snapchat originated the story-based format of sharing content online, which involved sharing a short video. This video disappears after a specific period. Snapchat has over 250 million users active, who all are there because of a variety of selling points offered by this platform. Some of them are using funny filters for selfie videos and photos, doodling, sending videos, and photos, etc. All these can be shared, which are then viewed by a user's friends.

Even though there have been reports that Snapchat has seen a decline in the users, it is still quite popular among young adults and teenagers. According to reports, 18 to 24 year olds are about 45% active on this platform. And, 76% teenagers among them are using Snapchat. If you have a product that involves a younger demographic, then it is a prudent idea to use Snapchat for your marketing campaign. If there has been a decline in this platform then it is mostly because other competitive platforms like YouTube, Facebook, and Instagram have also started implementing the tools used in Snapchat. And, the result is that the latter platforms are growing more aggressively.

Pinterest: The last social media platform that this book will discuss is Pinterest. This online portal is a place to get inspiration and to find new ideas for personal or professional aspect. Moreover, you have the ability to categorize them in various folders, which can be accessed to look into various innovations shared by over 200 million active users. The numbers still feel they are lower compared to other platforms, but it still is a huge number. Understand that Pinterest is the type of social media platform with one of the most influencing portals, just next to Facebook.

Pinterest is definitely a platform where you can look for great ideas. This means that people are likely to visit it to learn about new trends, brands, and artistry inventions. Over 93% of users (called as pinners) are involved in searching for new products on Pinterest. If you are involved in products with more than one versions, then you can choose it for gaining a decent following. It is also great for the ones who have a website or a blog running passively. You can end up gaining more traffic through Pinterest to your site, hence increasing your following and profits.

Chapter 2: Becoming An Influencer

Here is a plus point about involving in social media in the present time: there is someone present in the world, who made the error that you do not need to. You cannot only learn from your own marketing mistakes, but also from the ones that others made. By understanding the status of their influencer and business pages, you can understand what things work and what do not.

Influencers have specifically mastered this idea. These are becoming extensively popular nowadays, which is why they can be considered to be a great tool for your business plan. Do understand that you can implement the info offered here to become an influencer for your company. Moreover, you can also apply all this information to your business pages linked to any of your social media accounts.

For the ones who are still confused about what influencers are and the reason behind their popularity concerning business, please go through the following section.

Influencers are the individuals who are chosen by firms with a huge following over social media. These people have a considerable amount of influence over the followers of the company. They are hired by the firms to create posts for them on social media, which mostly is positive feedback or review related to a product or service. Such influencers share their views after experiencing the service or product for the companies. Eventually, positive feedback may influence the follower to try out that product or service as he or she trusts the reviews of the influencer. As a result, the follower purchases it.

Many people of such types can earn tons of dollars using this technique. For instance, such influencers may end up earning high by just posting a normal picture on Instagram endorsing a product of a company. Even a small tweet of

100 words is worth thousands of dollars for them.

Influencers can be very valuable for companies, as customers usually lose the trust upon brands and businesses that they use for shopping. Only 10% or less trust these corporations without being influenced by anyone's wordings. Moreover, the click-through rates of ad campaigns are also staggering nowadays.

That is when influencers are involved. By informing his or her hundreds of thousands of followers, an influencer can affect their minds. As a result, the followers end up buying the product or service, most probably because they see the influencer using it themselves. Such influencers have the right technique to make friends of their followers, and can help in boosting the revenue by simply recommending a product or service or offering a promo code. As people usually trust the people they like as a person, in this case an influencer, it becomes much easier for firms to sell their services and products.

In most situations, an influencer will not charge you a couple of thousand dollars for a post. Their price varies depending upon the level of engagement as well as the number of followings per post. Often you can avail an affordable option from them, which involves paying influencers for advertising based on large-scale. This can be a significant investment at your end if you feel an influencer will help you.

To implement their use as much as possible, you will first have to understand the way they operate. Plus, you will need to understand how they handle their operations. Furthermore, you can understand several other aspects of them, such as running your own business page. In short, it is never bad to admire the ideas and implementing them in your own business.

The Secret Behind Becoming An Influencer

As a beginner, you need to understand that influencers are quite cautious while choosing products and services to endorse. They carefully choose the products that they are passionate about or believe in.

While you will still find a few who will just collaborate with any firm that can offer money for supporting their product or service, most influencers do not focus on this careless strategy. First and foremost, they will ask of samples from the company to test the product themselves. They do this so that they know the authenticity and quality of the product before recommending it to their audience.

Most reputed influencers of 2019 would not bother promoting a bad product because they respect their followers too much, and they would never want them to end up buying a bad item. Moreover, they will also choose a niche they love. As a businessman, you will need to make sure that their niche of passion aligns with your business niche. You will learn more about it in detail in the upcoming chapter.

Everything that is present on their profile is solid,

as they cannot compromise with mediocre due to being a role model to thousands or millions of followers under their accounts. Their profile picture, their posts, and their bio, all information about them has to be the best they can offer. The key here is to attract the audience, which these influencers are capable of achieving with their style and personality. Plus, they will make sure that their information present on their social media accounts is relatable to the followers so that the people can feel connected to them at ground level in some way. This increases their faith in the influencer.

You can consider it similar to a fashion magazine, where you are continuously witnessing beautiful people showing off their high-quality apparel, bodies, and accessories. You will notice that such celebrities and models in these magazines frequently wear things that are not so practical for daily use. An influencer would take these clothes and accessories, and wear them in a way a normal person would wear them. This causes the followers to buy such items because now they can relate to them. Similarly, you can choose any item, and use the same idea as done in the previous example, to get a similar result out of it.

Their technique is to make a significant factor of engagement involving their followers. They reply to their queries, like the comments they post, and frequently execute polls on their social media profiles for the followers. Moreover, they will ask their followers to use hashtags, and offer with promo bonuses and other prizes if they do as they are told.

For a prudent influencer, the primary objective is not just being a relatable person with the followers, but also display that such aspects can be done in real life as well. They want to show their audience that fashion sense similar to magazine models can be implemented in real-world scenarios without being embarrassed. They want to show their followers that the person influencing them is not a branded façade meant to just earn, but an actual person involving in helping others by offering them the best product recommendations, which he or she wears too.

A prudent way influencers prefer doing it is by being as true to the audience as possible. They would talk about stories and incidents in their lives, so that the followers can understand who and what type of a person the influencer is. Such stories shared to the audience are in-depth so that it can help the person understand him or her better. Many times, they speak of other things, like their struggles and insecurities in life. If, in some way, they can add a promo code or product in their stories, then it is even more beneficial. Think of a fashion model who is mentioning about her struggles of life while talking to her audience. Will the audience not feel connected in that situation?

However, influencers do make sure that they do not connect too much with the followers at a personal level. Any type of post that they share online is carefully structured so that it is not too personal, but still is linked to the brand they promote. Another secret behind being an influencer is the image they build around them. They have to be very careful about that too, so that it is spotless of any negative impacts. They are aware that people follow them for the inspiration, the ideas, and the way they live their lives on screen. People will not care about how the influencer lives in real life, as that side is not that interesting. So, the influencer tries to show that side of his or her life that is perfect.

If an influencer owns a food blog, and he or she shares a post about his or her cat passing away, even though the cat had little to do with the blog, it can cause some subscribers to unfollow. However, do understand that the situation would have been much more influential if the cat, when alive, was mentioned regularly in the posts. In the end, you need to understand that the page's primary purpose is to promote the business.

Most businesses understand what the message is all about and what they actually are. However, it is an error that a number of influencers and businesses tend to make. They are not aware of what the message really is and what the purpose of having all those business pages is. Influencers will often choose a theme or topic, which relates to them, something that they are passionate about and they do not mind keeping that theme for their whole life. However, that passion should already exist which will really relate with your followers and not just you. You need to build a brand that will focus on the bigger picture and not just you if you care about your brand. Otherwise, your followers will not care about it either.

Influencers also make plans frequently. Here, the idea is to create posts in advance, sometimes weeks before the sharing of a post. They carefully select the most appropriate time for sharing such a post, which they add with filters and hashtags. They will review each of their posts, ensure that the posts are resonating with their social media theme page, and they will make sure that they only post things that their followers would love to see.

Influencers will also find ways to understand their social media pages completely. They will keep track of the analytics, the results, and all feedbacks given to their pages for staying extra careful about their brand's image. A skilled influencer will consistently search for new types of ideas on how to implement fresh ways, filters, hashtags, and other marketing things for getting more followers to their accounts. They will do this so that their content stays engaging at all times. They will do this to increase brand awareness. You should be applying such tactics to your business as well.

Influencers also do not hesitate to search for ideas by studying other influencers. Do note that this is probably the main reason most influencers started doing what they do in the first place. The used to watch other people do it, and then they became innovative and ended up creating their own social media platforms. Such businesses need to follow such models, and understand that there is already a person present in the world who did what you are trying to do. They are already aware if what they did was a mistake or not.

If you find an influencer who has the same kind of brand to yours, spend some time studying their profile. You may also select businesses that are mostly the same and study them for innovative tips. Make a note of how they post their content on their pages, learn about the type of posts they share online, find out which hashtags they are implementing in their posts, etc. You can consider it a part of market research, which you already should know is an important aspect of any type of marketing.

The Significance Of Sticking To Your Brand

Note that consistency is essential on every aspect of your business. You have to be constant with the product value, how the product works, and with the nature of your brand. The same principle applies to social media.

Frequent posts, which are on schedule, will be very valuable for building a reputation for your brand. It is an irreplaceable strategy that will help your brand spread its wings from its original platform. Changing it from time to time will involve you to do it from scratch to keep its influence among potential followers as high as possible.

Changing your brand often leads to confusion among followers as they do not understand what you are suggesting. Sometimes, the brand owner is also clueless about why they changed their brand image or marketing strategy. If your followers are not sure of what your brand stands for, then they might not feel connected with it. This may probably end up in you losing your followers as they do not feel the passion for following your brand anymore.

Thus, it is important that you locate the right balance between surprising your potential followers and being constant with your brand marketing approach. Changing your brand from time to time is fine, but do not do it completely, and that too all of a sudden, which will lead to you losing your following.

Note that by the end of the day, the secret to success in the marketing world is to stay constant with your approach. Do not let it be predictable as then your audience will not find any interest in following you and your brand. In other words, you should try to entertain your audience and surprise them from time to time, which will keep them glued to you and your work. It will offer you the love and passion you need for your work as well as from your followers.

If you are not even aware of what your brand is all about until now, then it's important that you know about it before proceeding with your strategies. You will learn more about it in the upcoming chapter where you will figure out the right way of knowing your audience, your niche, and your brand.

However, if you are already aware of what your

brand represents, then you can go through the following tips to help you maintain consistency to keep it new and interesting at all times in front of your audience.

- **Making simple and easy-to-understand guidelines**

You should always create a long list of guidelines, not just for the things that you can do for your business, but also for the things that you cannot do. If your company has a team for brainstorming sessions, then ensure that the team has the freedom to make such lists. Just make them understand the type of message you want to come up with for your followers.

- **Add your brand-based assets, always and as early as possible.**

If you have a motto or a tagline related to your brand, then make sure to use it as much as possible with your brand. You may have seen several brands using taglines, for instance Lays uses its tagline "No one can eat just one." Such slogans and taglines will help your followers connect and recall your brand easily as they will relate it with your brand.

- **Understand what had worked in the previous case, and apply it to a new idea you are going to implement.**

Think of it this way, how will you improve the quality of a chocolate cake without first trying it yourself? If you have already been involved in marketing campaigns before, then use the ideas from that campaign and try applying it to your new campaign. If you are still unsure of what or how to implement, then check other influencers and business pages. Look at what has worked for them and try to implement a strategy based on their experience.

Some Mistakes To Avoid As An Influencer

Here are some mistakes that you should know about involving influencers.

- **Not understanding the right type of**

objective before proceeding with a campaign.

Every marketing campaign involving the promotion of product or services has to have a clear objective in mind. This objective may comprise of creating brand awareness, communicating with people, or introducing a new product in the market. A number of marketers try to execute promotional tactics without understanding the true objective.

A prudent way to avoid it is provided here. You just need to gather your team and discuss together what you all really want to achieve from your brand campaign. Elaborate on what you require if the marketing campaign succeeds. Furthermore, discuss what can be the result if the campaign fails. You should also be clear about what the outcome is if there is no success or failure. Even if there is no evident turnout from your campaign, you should know how to approach such a situation. When your objective is clear, you can create your marketing campaign around that discussion. You can then create your success based on whatever objectives you have in mind.

- **Not understanding your audience.**

This one is a big mistake that you need to avoid. You need to understand your audience as clearly as possible. Plus, you need to understand at whom your marketing campaign is aimed. Is your aim to influence the younger generation? Are the parents you are targeting with your campaign? Perhaps you are focusing on teenagers. All these things about your audience should be clear in advance. Even if they are the older generation, you should know whom to target and whom you do not.

To learn about your audience, you need to understand your product. You should think of the type of individuals who you were perceiving while designing your product. Who do you think would purchase it? Who will enjoy using it? What truly relates to them? How will you interact with such people to make it more effective? By learning about your audience, you will know what exactly to speak about with them, and react accordingly.

- **Not realizing which platforms are best for your brand.**

Not every platform is the same. Plus, each platform has its own pros and cons. Every one of them is designed to be implemented in a particular way, and it depends on what your business focuses on. Only a few of them will serve your brand's purpose.

To avoid the errors, you will have to research thoroughly on a particular platform of your choice. In later chapters, you will learn this concept in detail so that you know how to choose the right social media platform for your business. You will learn the right way to use the platform with the right approach later.

- **Improper planning of the campaign.**

As mentioned earlier, planning is essential here. It can cause trouble for your campaign if you are not fully realistic about your plan. You need to understand how your plan will work in motion from start to finish beforehand. If you do not know the complete path of its execution, then you may end up running into a hurdle that you were not aware of before.

It is always a prudent idea to come up with innovative perceptions several days, weeks, months, or even years in advance. You should have your primary focus on new ideas. Do not hesitate to jot them down whenever they strike in your mind. This will keep you prepared for using them in time of need. If you feel that you are not used to this technique, then you can take help from social media apps that have such planning strategies. A good app that has been popularly used by many influencers is Hootsuite. You can find several other options as well.

- **Collaborating with influencers that are not fit for your niche.**

Surely a majority of influencers will first test and examine a product properly before showing their consideration to promote it, but there are some who are just in to make a quick buck through any offer provided to them. In some cases, you may find an influencer who is already passionate about your product and just wants to collaborate with you. Before choosing an influencer, you need to properly examine his or her online presence, reputation and personality to collaborate with him or her. You may never know that you ended up linking with the wrong person, who could ruin the image of your product as well. It could affect your audience in a negative way at times.

Just as an influencer tests products before deciding on talking about them, you should test the approaches of your shortlisted influencers as well. Your business and brand will affect the type of influencers you are collaborating with. You will have to evaluate whether the influencer is fit to work with your company or not. Above all, you will have to do your research involving the social media page of the influencer. He or she needs to have something similar to your product. Only then will it feel relevant to hire such a person.

- **Overestimating the influence of an influencer.**

Note that a large following of an influencer is not the primary factor. Large numbers do not usually have large effects on the audience all the time. It may be great if you are doing it for brand awareness, but for other goals being partial with this factor is not a good idea. Moreover, you may not know but some influencers buy followers to increase their following, so technically they are not actual followers who love the individual's work. Plus, most of those followers may just be bots or fake accounts created for the sole purpose of increasing following. That's it!

You are not going to get any prudent attention

from such an influencer. Your first perception while selecting such a person should be the relevance of the niche, rather than the numbers. You should focus on collaborating with individuals who have genuine influence over their audience, and who can understand your niche industry efficiently. If awareness is your goal, then you can stick with an influencer who has a large and real following.

To understand whether you are choosing the right person, focus on their rate of engagement, as for your information more followers can mostly lead to fewer chances of engagement than they actually deserve. People with a low number of followers, say 1000, have at least 15% rate of engagement, while the ones with larger than 1,000,000 may have a rate of engagement at only 2%. Just note that, in such case, less means more.

- **Not showing your personal self.**

A majority of social media sites have strict rules asking influencers to let their followers be aware of posted ads on their account pages. Such sites want the people to be aware that influencers are being paid for what they are doing, which is promoting a brand. Some influencers, however, take this step too far, where they just add the ad's embed code directly on the post or caption, which looks selfish and rude at times.

This is an error, which you need to avoid at all costs. Note that, the real objective of an influencer is to show that he or she is not apparently involved in just promoting a brand or service. His or her content should not look like it is being endorsed or promoted for a company. People feel offended at times and may misinterpret influencers in such situations. People find such ads annoying, but they have learned to ignore them as well. So, direct ads like these will not be a beneficial step for influencers.

As an audience, you will not directly want such ads to be visible in front of your screen. But, skilled influencers will create ads in such a way that they do not actually look like ads. They will use a balanced approach to show ads in the caption, but only after sharing their views and opinions related to the product, which they actually use at times. They will share a personal incident related to the product if they have to so that people can relate to them and purchase the product if they feel like using it.

- **Investing Too Much Money.**

Unfortunately, this is a common error that can be seen in many businesses. People just feel that investing in an influencer, who has a good reputation, will inevitably take their brand to success. However, this overestimation is a big mistake. You should take this step carefully and not use all your money to invest in influencers and social media marketing experts. Remember to first research about it. For that, you need to go through this whole book so that you do not end up making mistakes when dealing with this platform. Do not step in the boat with both feet at once without evaluating the depth of the ocean. Learn to take one step at a time, and invest smartly to get genuine and promising results.

Collaborating With Influencers

A big challenge that comes in the minds of many businesses is getting your name out in public. While campaigns that involve traditional tactics are worth trying out, they can be really expensive at times. This can be particularly daunting for the ones who are just starting a new business venture. For, them investing millions in marketing can be a burden and a foolish move.

Thus, it is essential to understand that at least collaborating with an influencer may provide you with some approach to counter the money problem. Influencers will not just help you with the promotion of your product, but they will also advocate for your products. Most of the times, they will skip a product they are unfamiliar with as they do not want their reputation to become dirty in the process. Their relationship with their huge following is essential for them. If they lose their followers' trust, then it can even end their careers.

That is why, it is vital that you need to choose someone who is going to genuinely advocate your product. You may have to provide your product as a sample (at times free) to such influencers, who will then use it and experience it before offering their feedback. You will have to create a relationship that benefits both parties mutually in this collaboration. You may even have to become their sponsors for a long-term relationship where they will help you out as much as you help them. It will not only help you get more traffic to your products, but also help the influencer gain more popularity overall.

You will also have to share each other's posts online on your social media pages for this to work. You can even talk about them in your posts so that your audience may recognize them as well. Collaboration between parties has to be mutual, where both of them benefit while helping each other grow.

This will also involve a strong and consistent communication between both parties so strengthen the relationship in business. Your objectives will have to be clear so that there are limited chances of disagreements later on.

Hope you have understood influencers now.

Chapter 3: Initiating An Online Business Implementing Social Media

Starting an online business by using social media can be challenging at times. This can be especially daunting for the ones who have never done it before in the past. Fortunately, this chapter will help you get started with it in 2019 without worrying about the competition or approach.

Locating Your Market And Niche For Your Brand

Before you initiate with any type of business, in any location, you should know what your business is about, and who would be your targeted audience. A niche is a location that is suitable for your business in improving productivity. Furthermore, it can get even hard if you do decide what your niche is all about. You may indulge yourself spending hours and hours of your time finding the right approach, but eventually you may not find anything productive or lucrative about your business model.

Your first approach should be to categorize your passions. If you are initiating with your own business, your chosen platform should be about something that you have interest or passion in. If your chosen niche is something that bores you easily, then it may not be the right one for you. It does not mean that your passion is the key to a successful business model, but you do need something to drive you towards meeting your end goals. You need something that will keep you moving on with your marketing campaign.

To search for your desired passion, you need to inquire yourself with the following questions:

- What do you enjoy doing in your free time?

- Is there any organization or club that you are associated with? What do you indulge in that club or what type of organization it represents?

- Which topics do you find enjoyable while learning?

- How do you picture yourself when doing something?

Once you have asked yourself such questions, you would have to research whether such questions will influence your market research. You will have to evaluate the type of problems your customers will experience, and ask yourself whether you can solve that problem for them or not. You may even have to indulge in conversations with potential customers to understand their problems face-to-face. A good way of doing that is by indulging yourself in forums and websites. Furthermore, you can search for keywords and find whether your desired niche is being discussed by others or not.

You may also want to check out your competition. Learn if they are also having a similar product for their customers. If that is a possibility, then you will have to come up with a better option to lure in your customers. You may also want to create a list of points covering the rights and wrongs done by your competition. Rivalry in business may seem like a bad thing, but it is a prudent factor to get better at your business. You will have the opportunity to witness what your rivals are doing wrong in their business strategies and then implement the right approach to avoid those mistakes in your business model. This is quite crucial in 2019, as you can find a lot of competition. However, most businesses will not be able to have a full-fledged idea to improve their productivity online on social media platforms. If you feel like your rivals are not doing something good, then try to execute it in a better way.

You may even have to involve in certain tests. It might take some of your time to evaluate the niche you are targeting, but eventually it will be a prudent idea to do so. Do note that there is no flawless process to achieve your targets using social media but you can still avoid the mistakes that others are making. Many times, your best approach is to influence others with your reputation initially and then start with the selling of your products. You should never worry about the trivial parts, but do not forget to learn from your mistakes. Often, it is most crucial to popularize your name and learn from the research that you have done to create the perfect brand.

Locating And Stacking Your Customer Base

Firstly, you should analyze the objective and targeted audience of your product.

Ask yourself a question like: who will your product be targeted at?

Such a question is what startups ask themselves when starting. Plus, one should also understand whom your products will be sold to.

You can find this out by researching a number of aspects. These include family status, relationship status, career, race, gender, location, age and other similar aspects based on demographic locations. The list can be pretty long if you are willing to research deeply into this. If you already have potential customers, then you should be evaluating them as close as possible to determine who these consumers are, what profession do they have, and what are they planning to purchase from you. Understanding your customer base will give you the freedom to aim at finding more such people, thus increasing the number. In such a situation, you will have the advantage of knowing what type of product your customers want.

If you are still not sure about what type of target audience you have yet, or you have still not started selling yet, it is high time that you learn about it. If you are aware of your niche market already, then your first option will be to evaluate your competition. Who will be buying from you? Whom are your products marketed towards?

Understand your product as closely as possible. You need to figure out your product as deeply as possible. Plus, you need to keep track of the time you take to list your products as well. When you have all this figured out, then inquire yourself about the type of person who will benefit from your products or services. Create a list, and make sure to target such demographics.

Note that by demographics, you are targeting several things to filter out the most relevant of searches for your business. Surely factors like occupation, marriage status, family status, education level, income level, race, location, gender, and age are great factors to execute your plan initially, but there is a bigger picture involved in this scenario. And, often businesses ignore looking deeply in this field. Your potential customer also has lifestyle and characteristics, which are surely important. These comprise of aspects such as behavior, hobbies, interests, values, attitude, and ways to lead life to the fullest.

Here is an example to understand it:

Think of a situation where you are selling an application involving filters for cameras in smartphones. You may feel like targeting this smartphone app at the young generation, most probably at teenagers. However, note that all young people may not be having a use for such an app. So, you may have to think of a different approach to make people use your app. You may have to ask yourself various questions such as when and how will the users use this app? Which features will appeal to such users? How will it target their everyday lives? What type of hobbies and interest will they have, and will the app offer them more interest in the scenario or not? You will need to indulge in such questions before making your business plan.

Once you have it all figured out efficiently, you will need to evaluate your decision properly. You may need to understand whether there are enough users who require such an app, whether such an app will have an advantage in their lives or not, or if they will be able to afford it. You need to understand how your users feel about your proposed product by thinking just like them.

Furthermore, understand this: do not involve in breaking down your target audience too much. Instead you can counter such a situation by focusing on more than one group who are interested in your product. You can focus your marketing strategy at such groups individually, and still get effective results.

Sometimes structuring your target audience can be challenging on social media platforms. However, once you come to know this, it becomes simpler to create videos, images, and posts that your audience will love to see. After that, it is time to create an account.

Initiating Social Media

Once you have understood everything about targeting your audience, it is time to start building your social media account(s).

Starting your online business is quite similar to starting a business in the real world. Firstly, you should understand that some information that you will see here will be there online. But, most of the information is scattered on various sites, which can be hard to find and research at times. That is why, this book is your guide to understand it all in one place.

Fortunately, setting yourself up on social media is not that hard as people think of it to be. Most of the time, it involves engaging yourself with the audience by offering them what they were present for.

Furthermore, as stated before, you should always start with a prudent plan. Any prudent strategy involving business should comprise of a starting and ending point that has been thought of properly. Understand that a plan is a base that you will need in any business. Your plan will guide you carefully so that you stay focused at all times. Many businesses perceive that social media marketing does not involve much money-spending, so it must be simple to do. However, that is not how things work in this business. You need to have a plan first.

Your plan will help you understand where you are moving forward and what will your social media marketing techniques result in. Here is a list of tips that will help you understand what you need to do to make sure you are on the right path.

- **Understand what you need.**

What is your purpose for your social media account? Are you looking forward to luring more customers? Do you want your present customers to be aided through your direct involvement in their issues? What is the level of engagement you expect from each of your updates, and how do you plan to reach that level?

- **Go for an audit if you have to.**

If this is your first time with social media, and you feel like you are confused whether you are on the right track or not, then you may want to get our page audited. You can take help from many people online, who are experts in this. They will be able to check out your page and guide you for possible errors. Furthermore, you can just look for online sources that have checklists comprising of how your social media account pages should look like. With proper evaluation, you can have a way learning new ideas, understanding what is wrong, and finding ways to do the right thing. That way, you can move forward on the right track.

- **Inspire yourself from other sources.**

In fact, your inspiration sources should not just be limited to online portals. You can even inspire yourself looking at the accounts of your competition, influencers, other businesses, etc. Even if the business has nothing to do with your niche can inspire you at times. Research them thoroughly and try avoiding the mistakes they have made while implementing such ideas.

- **Learn the importance of consistency.**

Consistency involves posting as frequently as you can. It not only involves what type of post you are sharing, but also how often you are planning to post it. Remember that, people are influenced by you and following you because you interest them. Do not lose their interest in you. You need to regularly post interesting content so that people keep following you.

- **Research all potential social media platforms to find out the best one for you.**

You may need to involve yourself in demographic research. Try not to assume things on your own involving people and their preferred social media websites. You may never know what they are interested in unless you research about it religiously.

Once your pages are up on social media, then you need to start focusing on creating relationships.

Note that your followers should understand you more than just mere

followers. Your followers should be people who want to communicate with you, act as your partners, or should be your friends. Such a relationship will help them engage with you. People may not find it much effective, but at the end of the day, the few followers who liked, commented, and shared your posts are definitely much better than the ones who did not do anything to support you.

Strengthen your relationships by engaging better with individuals. The key here is to answer their queries, reply to their comments, follow them back, and give the people more than one reason to support you. Moreover, you need to aim at aiding your customers and followers, instead of just selling your products to them. No doubt, you need to run your business, but you do not want them to think that you do not care about them. Plus, you need to figure out ways to add more value to their lives for better support. The more involvement you have with your customer as a friend, the better chances there are for them to purchase a product from you.

Plan the posts skillfully. Similar to marketers, you need to plan your ads days, weeks, or even months beforehand. You need to plan your posts in this way for getting the best benefits. For instance, if you are entering the month of December, then you should have at least 20 posts ready to be published that is linked to Christmas content. If you focus on planning it ahead of your schedule, then you will never feel depleted of content to post on your social media pages. There will always be something available to share online with your followers in such cases.

Promote content through all your social media accounts. Several businesses indulge in multiple social media accounts, and they have a website. It is essential that you mention all your accounts every day. Fortunately, a number of social media accounts function more efficiently together. You can often incorporate a plan where you share several posts on all your accounts simultaneously. This cross-platform social media marketing can have its own unique benefits. For instance, Instagram comprises a feature where a user can share a post on Twitter and Facebook automatically.

Make sure to keep yourself active on your social media accounts. Having an account that is inactive for too long may result in the death of your brand before it even started online. Why would anyone bother to follow you if you are not even posting anything online? Surely, the number of posts published in a day or week is based on platform to platform, but you should still post at least once every day. People who have followed you want to know what your brand is up to. So, you might want to help them connect with you through this tip.

Be sentimental. Social media sites are all about being personal with others. Most users present there will indulge in personal communications, which are not biased by corporations. That is what the skilled influencers do. They involve themselves with their followers and become their friends. Note that a majority of such influencers are genuinely making friends with their followers. The money comes on itself. They laugh together, reply to queries of their fans, and acknowledge the comments posted on their social media pages. Overall, they are sentimental with them, which is the key to gain their trust. As a company, you will have to gain the trust of your followers by genuinely caring for their needs and not simply creating marketing pages for earning profits.

Setting Up Your Profile

It is crucial to have a profile on any of your social media platforms. It is the very first thing that any buyer or follower will witness when looking at your work. Concerning videos and photos, it is particularly significant because these have to be in the same color layout and theme for gaining a unique image. Note that your profile acts as your unique selling point, which will comprise of ideas you have thought to attract more followers.

Here is a way to explain this: If you have loved a

particular pair of jeans your whole life, will you try to go to a store to buy a new type of jeans unless really necessary? Surely not, as you already are aware of your choice of jeans. So, you may never try to grab a different pair. So, why would you waste your time going through other pairs, unless there is something interesting about a new pair.

Similarly, your profile needs to be attractive enough to make people like your content and posts. Moreover, each post that you publish will have to be more appealing than the previous one to achieve this.

Knowing what keywords are

A keyword is a word or group of words that an individual types into a search bar to find relevant results for it. Every business website has a number of keywords listed in their content online. Many businesses may not even be utilizing keywords skillfully, or maybe they are not choosing the appropriate ones.

People use keywords to search for things online every time. Just think about it: how often do you search for something on a search engine like Google? Most probably, at least ten times every day. The searching trend has even made Googling an actual verb and people are aware of it.

As keywords are important, you need to understand their use and implement them even on your social media account pages. To start it, you need to first create a list of relevant words and phrases that you feel have something to do with your website. Then you can use them in your posts as often as you can. Here is an example: If you are involved in cake-making business, and you are sharing a new type of cake recipe, then you can use words like "recipe," "cake," and "bake."

The Significance Of Tone And Consistency

It is important to maintain consistency in any type of business. One needs to keep a consistency in quality, consistency in advertising, and overall consistency of the product. A similar protocol is acknowledged in the social media platform as well.

Note that consistency is not limited to just the frequency of posting an update on your social media page or developing your brand. Additionally, it focuses on the personality and tone as well. Try thinking of your friends in a scenario. How will it feel to see them changing their interests and personality every other day? You may not want to be friends with such people anymore, as you will have little idea of how they would react in any situation. Above all, you may start disliking that person because they may not be the same individual in personality anymore.

Furthermore, your tone related to social media is also essential. If you have a brand that is silly and playful, then you need to make sure that your brand has such a vibe. If you have a brand that is specific to a point, then you should create posts that have that feel. It will enable your audience to learn about what your business is all about. They will recognize your more often and will understand the purpose of your products and company.

It may be a challenging task: searching for a method to interact with your followers, which feels authentic. Plus, relating to your audience is the key, and you will have to stay transparent with them to gain their trust.

For followers to understand and familiarize with your brand or niche, they need to witness the things that you post on your social media pages. If you keep on posting about a different niche every time, your audience may get confused about the specific niche that you target. If your posts are limited to one or two every few weeks, they may not even follow you anymore. They will feel that you do not care about them and do not intend to stay connected with them. With every post that you update, you have an opportunity to interact with your audience and make them feel connected to you.

Your consistency needs to resonate in every

portion of your page on the social media platform. Even your tone in all your posts should be direct and unique. Whenever you will share anything related to some other business's social media page, that something will have to be in harmony at one level or other with your brand. You should also note that it is crucial to think about the information and the source. Never feel confused when thinking of checking some information, which you find online, twice. Even checking for facts will help you in using relevant content for your brand.

Lastly, you need to always note that every post, which you create for your social media campaigns, has a visual connection with each other. You will have to focus on improving the appearance of your complete profile. A majority of people feel attracted to visual representation. All parts of the content, which includes video posts to header images, need to connect together to display the whole scenario of the campaign. You can experiment with various formats to achieve your desired profile. Note that adding variety to your marketing strategy will make your audience stay interested in your content, which may indulge them to try out your products or services.

This book will now cover a separate chapter focused on popular social media platforms, which you may feel like using. You will have the information needed to focus on strengthening your profile. You will achieve this by engaging with your followers using the best type of posts. Note that this is just a small part of your social media marketing tactic. Now, let us move to the next chapter that will focus on monetizing your audience in 2019.

Chapter 4: Monetizing Your Audience In 2019

To remind you again, the absolute purpose of this book is to help you Make Money. After all, that was the main reason you chose this book, isn't it? Thus, now we will come to the question that has been in the mind of any type of business: How can you monetize your online business?

Revenue generation with consistency is the main reason why several businesses have entered the world of social media. They had a need of choosing this platform so that they could connect with new people, who may turn out to be potential customers. This could eventually lead to selling more services and products, and offering more opportunity to earn money. So, without a doubt the ultimate objective is to earn cash.

However, once your audience tends to buy the product, or like your posts, or follow your content, how are you earning? How are you making sure that your followers are attracted to your work? How are you indulging your customers in buying products from you for more than once?

Fortunately, if people are following your content online, then you have accomplished half of your goals, so be proud of that! People are already interested in and invested in your online content. Now, all you have to do is make them be aware of your services or products meant for selling. If they are following you and your methods of living, then it would be much easier to make them buy your products.

You have already climbed half the steps. So, your next goal is to make them climb up to the top to engage in buying what you have for them.

- **Direct Sales**

If a follower directly messages you to inquire about some product or service that you deal in, then you should not hesitate to connect with him or her. Note that you do not show your ego by not messaging him or her, as you may think that that person messaged you from a social media account. Being directly involved with your customers through social media's direct messaging tools will give you a better edge at gaining their trust.

Moreover, in this situation, you can even offer them in-depth information about the product, its benefits, and sales pitches about it if you have to. And, all that is possible right from your phone or computer. So, even though your customer might be situated overseas, communicating with them personally will ensure that your customer connects with you more often to inquire about your products and services.

- **Posting the reviews that are positive**

The Internet has revolutionized our lives and shopping scenarios. If any person buys something online today, then he or she usually gets back to post a review on the same. Therefore, if you get any positive reviews about your product, then you must quote them as they are. This helps in letting other potential customers know that your product is wanted and that they might need it too. Either you can post the reviews as quotes in pictures or you can also feature your satisfied customers with permission. This helps to garner positive publicity.

- **Make customers aware of new products and offers**

Just merely evolving and bringing new ideas and products into the market does not ensure that they will be sold. Therefore, one must bring those new products to the customers who already follow you as somewhere they are already in alignment with the core with which your products are made. Along with the customers, you must also let your followers know as well as they are the potential customers. You need to engage a thought that your new product could promise to fulfill their need. This push would be necessary enough for them to buy your products. Hence, you must post about the latest developments.

- **Provide discounts to your customers**

Discounts always gather the attention of your customers. You must provide them with some nice discount offers, like providing your product at 40 percent off to the first 100 hundred buyers or giving them vouchers on their first purchase. Deals like this are hard to resist. Big companies tend to make a lot of profit by hosting such discount offers where a certain number of people who tend to be first will get amazing discounts. Providing a discount is a way in which you can widen the base of your loyal customers. Discounts are a form of appreciation for your customers who tend to be loyal to you.

- **Offer free samples**

Getting free samples is always attractive to customers. This helps them to understand the nature, taste, benefits or features of your product personally at hand. Getting to experience the actual product can boost your sales because if a person really likes it, then he might just buy it at the same moment. Free samples give an idea of how your product is and instills an amount of trust in the customer. When you want to sell something online, like a book, then you can offer the first two or three chapters of it to your customers as a sample. If they find it interesting enough, then they would buy it for sure.

- **Try giving tutorials**

Doing tutorials and showing them to your customers makes them realize the flexibility of your product. They get to the various ways in which the product that you are offering can be used. For example, if your product is a couch cum bed, then you must show them how easily they can convert this couch into a bed and relax. Alternatively, if your product is a food item, then the easiest to show your customers is to how it can be used in various recipes. Tutorials always keep your followers engaged with the usage of your product.

- **Create appealing content**

Most often, the mistake done by the businesses online is that the content through which they promote their products is boring or not interesting at all which is why it fails to serve the purpose of increasing the sales. Dry content does not contribute to your sales or its improvement in any way. Therefore, you must try to strengthen your content, which will attract potential customers for you and contribute to your aim of increasing sales. Once your content is good, then your followers might be motivated to share it and gather more support.

- **Post blogs and articles to generate ad revenue**

You can develop your content through blogs and articles. You can also share that content on all your social media platforms. This will attract more audience to your content, which will be influenced to invest in your products. The most basic thing to be taken care of is that the title and the cover images must be of good quality. This will help you to generate ad revenue, which is a part of sales.

Chapter 5: Marketing With Facebook

A recent report on social media has revealed that about 93.7% of businesses are actively marketing on Facebook. This is a new revelation for people who thought that Facebook marketing had no future after 2018.

Facebook is a strong platform, which will be used for marketing online by businesses across the globe. So, it would be wise for you to prepare a penetrating Facebook marketing strategy aligned with the trends of 2019.

Facebook Trends You Can't Ignore In 2019

- **Videos impress audiences the most**

Whether you want a strategic renewal or want to make a fresh Facebook strategy in 2019, don't forget to include video content. The engagement level on videos is exceptionally higher than any other kind. Almost 60 percent higher engagement is achieved by videos on Facebook these days.

On the contrary, the posts with links and images don't get as many engagements.

- **Most popular content types include funny, inspirational and practical**

Diving into the specific content types, you should try to target an inspirational, funny or practical approach. These content types have gained maximum attention on Facebook in recent times. Funny and inspirational content receive the maximum reactions of "love" and "HAHA".

You can easily transform your current marketing strategy into these content types. Simply understand how your audiences react to different content types and incorporate the conclusions.

- **Facebook shop ensures conversions for businesses**

Having a vast community on Facebook won't ensure ROI if you are not using the Facebook shop yet. A Facebook shop allows your consumers to easily find what they wish to obtain. E-commerce businesses are utilizing functional plugins to integrate online store with their Facebook page.

A Facebook shop is the ultimate solution to keep your community intact. This is extremely important as every business looks for conversions through every marketing effort. The shop works as a convenient medium for Facebook audiences to become a customer. The products, as well as services, stay present and accessible for Facebook audiences. They can make a simple click and see all your offerings on a single page.

Managing a Facebook shop is easy too. The shop stays aligned with your online store. So, whenever you make modifications in your store, it automatically updates those modifications on your Facebook shop as well. This way, you don't have to worry about eliminating or adding products twice every time. One inventory modification fixes the second Facebook inventory as well.

With the Facebook shop, you also become more aware of the sales happening via the social media platform. The analytics informs how many visitors turn into customers. This helps in understanding the ROI you are attaining.

- **Facebook ads deliver targeted exposure**

There is a huge diversity in terms of Facebook ad objectives. If you have a product or a service to market in 2019, advertising on Facebook would be a great addition in your strategy.

Investing in ads on Facebook gives you the ability to run interest-based and result-oriented ads. You choose the exposure quality in advance. This allows you to invest the most needed amount and get strong performance for your business. You can utilize metrics to ensure that every campaign performance as per your benchmarks.

In the gist of every marketing strategy, the goal is

to find interested customers and make them loyal to your brand. And this is exactly what you achieve with Facebook ads. The ads reach groups of users who actually look for products and services you sell. These people get a chance to know about your product, interact with your business and obtain the products as well. This cycle of purchase can lead to thousands of new loyal customers for your business. These loyal customers keep on coming again and again for your products.

We will discuss detailed Facebook ad strategies in the next chapter.

- **Facebook stories and Facebook Live deliver immediate results**

If your goal is to increase awareness, get more likes and drive traffic, Facebook Live and FB stories are incredible choices to target. While stories appear right on the top section of the users' Facebook page, live videos enable two-way communication in real-time. Businesses are utilizing these features to launch their new products, showcase product performance and answer customer queries as well.

Facebook stories are also effective when you launch season-based discounts or want to showcase customer stories or testimonials.

How To Make A Winner Facebook Marketing Strategy In 2019?

We have examined the most important Facebook marketing trends for 2019. Now, let's understand how you can incorporate these trends to make your Facebook marketing strategy successful.

Even if you are simply starting to market your business on Facebook, the following tips will help you build and implement scalable strategies this year.

1. Align Facebook strategy with core business goals

With the huge availability of opportunities, it is easy to divert from the focused path on Facebook.

You easily feel overwhelmed by the vastness of the platform. Saving your business from this is possible only if your strategies are intact with core business goals.

You need to choose specific goals that align with your current and future business objectives.

•   If you are simply starting your business, you would want to increase the awareness, increase Facebook likes, followers and obtain site traffic. So, you can align these goals with your Facebook marketing strategy and post quality posts frequently. You need to set up a Facebook page and obtain higher benchmarks of engagement gradually. For instance, you can decide to obtain 300 likes every month and decide to post at least 3 posts every week.

•   In case you have an upcoming event to promote, an event page on Facebook becomes a targeted strategy. The goals for an event is to obtain as many attendees as possible. But you should decide a specific number of attendees to target. This way, you can decide ad investment per new attendee.

• For an e-commerce store, business goals are mostly about getting more customers and increasing profits. To achieve that, you can target conversion-based Facebook ad campaigns. You will need to constantly monitor the cost invested for every conversion and ensure a high ROI. The metrics provided on Facebook Ads Manager will help you do that.

If you are still confused and don't know how to begin, ask yourself these questions:

• What has your business achieved last year? How do you want to upgrade those achievements this year?

• Do you want to attain short-term or long-term results from Facebook?

• How is your business different from your existing competitors? How can you present that differentiation on Facebook?

With the obtained answers, you will know your core business goals. And they will help you create a Facebook marketing strategy with specific and relevant goals.

2. Evaluate your existing Facebook posting habits and behavior

If you have a Facebook page, go and look at the content types you have been posting. Also, notice the content pieces that gained maximum reactions, comments and/or shares.

While doing this, you should think about two things:

•   Is there a trend related to your Facebook posting habit?

•   Are particular content types getting more engagement?

Each user on Facebook showcases his or her story with the world. They share, like and comment on posts that align with their interests and values. Marketers and businesses need to understand those values and interests. They can change with respect to different demographics. Hence, it will require an in-depth analysis of your target market. Your business needs to align with the personalities and stories of your target audiences.

To achieve harmony with your Facebook audiences, you need to constantly experiment and improve marketing strategies. The interests change on a personal level and it also changes on a community level. Which is why you need to constantly look at internal as well as external factors of your audiences' personality change.

When trying to understand your market, it is common to come across multiple groups. This creates convenient segments you would want to target on Facebook. Your marketing strategy can have different sections, targeting different segments of the target market.

Facebook provides Audience Insights to help you understand your demographics without spending a lot of money. The tool is free and you can understand demographics, page likes, location, activity and various other insights related to your audiences. Within minutes, you can understand how many men or women follow your business page, check out the dominating age group and know the location of your audiences as well.

So, how to use this data in your marketing strategy?!

The obtained data from Audience Insights becomes helpful in making a list of posts that most demographics enjoy watching. You can visit competitor pages to see the content types they promote to impress the similar types of audiences. Hence, you never feel out of post ideas or become irrelevant to your audiences.

The process is surely not a one-time success formula. You can research regularly, generate new ideas, try them in your marketing strategy and learn from your mistakes.

3. Make Facebook campaigns human and

mission-driven

Shallow marketing isn't working in 2019. More than 84% of marketers on Facebook believe in standing up for something and building long-term trust among audiences. This is how brands will survive this year and beyond. Consumers are interacting with brands that have a purpose. Businesses that run campaigns with a human approach, win the maximum response.

You have to be authentic, real and target human stories to engage audiences. Let people see real-life stories to connect with your brand. This type of marketing is possible for smaller brands as well. You can ensure a personal approach in every campaign to engage your audiences with a cause.

For instance, you can highlight the people who work behind your brand and tell their stories. The human-centered stories receive more shares, reactions, comments, and video views as well. This is due to the emotional impact that real stories bring to the marketing campaigns.

Make this concept essential for every campaign and include other features such as chat bots, Facebook messenger, Facebook group and/or Facebook shop.

4. Find a balance of short-lived and long-term Facebook marketing approach

Social media has changed right in front of all of us. The increased use of mobile devices, reduction in attention span and higher influence of new age generation. These reasons have increased the popularity of short-lived content. The trend is still going on in 2019 and it presents great marketing opportunities for businesses.

You can run niche, active groups and nourish them with short-lived content such as Facebook Live and stories. However, the same platform allows you to build communities that last for years and stay with your brand. The power of community is still important on social media, as it strengthens your brand's authority in the digital world.

The challenge here is to find the correct balance of short-lived content and long-term marketing approach. Here are the steps you can take:

Step 1 – Some posts should be free from commercial goals such as traffic or sales. This will make your posts more human-oriented and interesting. So, people won't think that you are trying to sell something to them all the time.

Step 2 – With the first step, you can easily increase the level of interactions and conversations with audiences and customers. This is exactly what the second step is all about. It is your responsibility to make these interactions satisfactory and memorable for your audiences whenever they engage. This will increase the word-of-mouth around your Facebook presence.

Step 3 – The third step is all about playing the long-term game and gradually increasing the awareness and authenticity of your brand. This will take time and you have to be persistent. Keep delivering engaging posts and solutions and the change will happen.

5. Make a video marketing strategy for Facebook

If images equal a thousand words, videos tell a million words these days. The biggest part of Facebook marketing involves video content. From ads to posts, videos provide the maximum business for brands. About 57 percent of consumers have admitted purchasing products after watching a video. It is obvious as well-designed videos make it easy for consumers to understand products and concepts. Images surely fall behind in that department. A video conveys the message faster. So, launching a new product or service is better with videos to ensure that consumers understand everything.

To make an effective Facebook video marketing strategy, you need to consider the following factors:

Video length: When using videos for ads, you should tap into the short zone of video length. With 15-30 seconds of video length, you can achieve the maximum watch time on your video. Most consumers will see the whole video. This won't be possible with a long video ad. Viewers will leave after half the message and won't follow the call-to-action. If you go beyond 30 seconds of video length, include your CTA after half of the video ad. You can make longer videos to post on your business page or group. The length can vary with respect to the story you want to tell. Just make sure it is engaging and aligning with your audiences' interest.

Sound quality and subtitles: About 85% of viewers watch Facebook videos without switching on the sound. But that doesn't mean you should focus on the quality of video sound. You simply need to integrate subtitles to effectively convey your message. Subtitles and high-quality sound together ensure that your video content becomes consumable for all kinds of audiences. You can use interesting fonts and highlighted text to let audiences read the message while watching the video. This also helps when you want to target audiences on a global scale.

Video format: Facebook users access videos on different devices such as smartphones, tablets, and laptops. So, you need to select a video format that aligns with all screen sizes. Choosing a square format is the best possible choice. However, you can also deliver videos in vertical formats.

Video content: The most important aspect of video marketing is the content type you select. As discussed before, you can't focus only on selling your brand and product. It should be the underlined idea only. First, you should incorporate the emotions that your audiences respond to. Using that idea, you can make videos about a product or service explanation, customer stories, behind the brand, and other creative content.

Now, you have a comprehensive understanding of how to market your business on Facebook in 2019. But wait, there is one more aspect that requires detailed understanding. Let's discuss how to utilize Facebook ads in the next chapter!

Chapter 6: Facebook Ads

Most people don't pay attention to television ads, they definitely don't care about ads in newspapers and magazines. This low attention is the reason why ad space on these platforms is highly overpriced.

On the other hand, there is Facebook with interest-based and goal-oriented ad campaign opportunities. They allow businesses to run ad campaigns at budget-friendly costs. At the same time, the reach and conversion rate are far better than traditional forms of advertising.

Again, it all comes down to how you prepare a Facebook ad strategy. This chapter will prepare you in every aspect such as setting ad objectives, leveraging different kinds of ads and other steps required in 2019.

Every Ad Campaign Objective You Can Find On Facebook In 2019

First and foremost, you should decide a clear

objective for your ad campaigns on Facebook. This way, Facebook optimizes your whole campaign around the objective you wish to accomplish. The algorithms look for the audiences in your target zone, who are most likely to respond to the ad.

Facebook keeps updating the number of objectives in their list. The most important ones in 2019 include:

For awareness:

- Reach

- Brand Awareness

For consideration:

- Post Engagement

- Traffic

- Page Likes

- App Installs

- Event Responses

- Lead Generation

- Video Views

- Messages

For conversion:

- Catalog Sales

- Conversions

- Store Visits

Let's discuss them all in detail!

1. Brand awareness

This campaign objective presents your ad to people who can easily recall. Facebook algorithms find people who invest maximum time period watching ads. Then, your ads reach those people for maximum outcome. This objective is perfect when you want to gain audience attention and enhance the talk around your product and services.

2. Reach

When you choose "Reach" as your campaign objective, Facebook focuses on sending your ad to as many people as possible in your target market. You decide the budget for your campaign. Depending on the budget, people see your ads once or multiple times. The idea is to gain as many eyes as possible to spread the message.

3. Post engagement

When you want to obtain more likes, increase comments and/or shares, post engagement becomes the right objective. On Facebook, the number of likes, shares and comments increase the social proof of your brand's popularity. Audiences tend to decide their attention span depending on the number of shares and comments they see on posts. This objective allows you to reach out to audiences that are warm and like to engage on social media.

4. Traffic

This objective has been designed to drive traffic

to websites. You can use this objective to obtain link clicks and increase traffic on your blog. However, don't utilize traffic objective to obtain conversions. For that, you should concentrate on conversion objectives.

5. Page likes

This objective is clearly all about getting more likes on your business page on Facebook. But it is important to understand the importance of page likes. Don't target page likes because you want to increase your organic reach of posts. Most people who like your page don't usually respond to all the posts. The main purpose of getting more likes is to improve social proof. Even if an individual likes your content, he or she will look at the number of likes on your page to decide your popularity.

6. App installs

If you have an app to promote, this campaign objective can help. It allows people to click and reach the download location. This increases the number of installs and also improves the rankings of your app. You can decide on a suitable budget to run such campaigns for a few days.

7. Event responses

For event promotion, you can target this objective. Selecting this will send your event ad to people who fit the right age group, have interest and live in the same location. In many situations, you can include this objective as a small part of your overall marketing strategy.

8. Video views

You have read all about the importance of promoting your business via video content. You can make video ads and choose this objective to engage the maximum possible views. Almost every business owner and marketer are utilizing this objective in 2019 to run video ads. It helps you obtain leads, traffic, sales or any other call-to-action you desire from your target audiences.

9. Lead generation

With lead generation, you get to collect important data such as name, phone number, email address and more. You can use this objective to enhance your collection of prospects and their personal information.

Every time a viewer clicks on such an ad, he or she receives a contact page provided inside the Facebook platform. The person then fills out the form to obtain services from your business.

This objective will align with your business if you provide services and want to reach out to your local consumers. Facebook makes convenient and easy forms to help people fill them quickly.

Now, it is important that you connect with your prospect as soon as you receive the contact. Otherwise, they will forget about your business and lose interest.

10. Messages

You can run ads on Facebook Messenger and

begin conversations using this objective. In 2019, this is another essential approach you should incorporate into your Facebook marketing strategy.

This objective allows you to utilize Facebook Messenger in two ways. First of all, you get to advertise your products and services. However, this should not be the only purpose, or it will create a bad reputation among target audiences. The second goal is more effective and beneficial from a business point. It is the opportunity of starting a conversation with consumers. The conversation leads to increased clicks. Hence, you win more prospects.

Services and products, both can be promoted via messenger. If your services or products cost a lot of money, consumers are more likely to assess a lot before buying. That is when you can leverage Facebook Messenger along with "messages" objective.

11. Catalog sales

Suppose you have a large group of people who are interested in your product or service. In that case, you would want to show them the collection of your products. Such collections are called catalogs, which contain product information. You can advertise your catalogs using this objective. The ad reaches the relevant people and increases the chances of sales.

Facebook allows you to connect your catalog from an online platform. Then, you can retarget audiences who are most likely to make a purchase.

12. Conversions

Every smart Facebook advertiser uses this objective to ensure a high ROI out of every campaign. After all, conversion is what every business requires from ad campaigns. This objective combines multiple goals to pick from. Depending on your conversion goals, you can choose "add to cart", "leads", "purchases", "view content" and other types of conversions.

To target sales and leads, you can choose purchases. You will have to install Facebook Pixel on your official website to run these types of ad campaigns. Also, you will have to install the desired event code such as purchases, leads and more.

With this initial effort, you can design your campaigns with specific and valuable conversions.

13. Store visits

This objective smoothly integrates your offline marketing objectives with the online objective. These days, your store visits begin with online interaction. People ask questions, get information, then, decide to visit the store.

This objective lets local consumers know about your business and its location. This increases the number of store visits.

Facebook Ad Types and How To Use Them

1. Photo ads on Facebook

Photo ads are the simplest form of advertisement you can run on Facebook. You can pick a concept-based image and incorporate a CTA to make your ad effective.

•   Make sure you select a compelling image concept that generates interest and aligns with your purpose.

•   Avoid blurry images and choose the maximum possible resolution.

•   Try to include as little text as possible.

2. Video ads on Facebook

Video ads will always impress you with their higher reach, engagement as well as conversions.

•   Grab viewers' attention with interesting thumbnail and title.

•   Make the first 2 seconds as interesting as

possible.

• Keep your video ads 15 to 30 seconds long.

• Choose a mobile-friendly format for maximum views.

• Keep the video resolution as high as possible.

• Include subtitles so people can watch videos on mute as well.

• Try 360-degree view videos to gain more attention.

3. Slideshow ads on Facebook

With slideshows, you can promote a group of images or videos. It also decreases the budget of running an ad campaign. You can target low-bandwidth zones with image slideshows to allow audiences to see your message.

4. Carousel ads on Facebook

A carousel ad incorporates different product

images as well as videos. A viewer can swipe to see the products. Every slide contains a CTA such as subscribe, call now and 16 others. You can incorporate objectives such as leads, store visits or conversions with this ad type.

• You should use multiple slides to showcase your range and create a brand story.

• Use relevant, meaningful and complementing images to enhance your brand story.

• Include the best images or products in the initial slides.

5. Collection ads on Facebook

Collection ads are great to provide an instant experience of your brand to consumers. Usually, such ads contain the best images along with a video. You can use this type of ad with objectives such as conversions, sales or traffic.

With collection ads, you can provide an instant storefront showcasing your best products. You can tell your brand story with a Lookbook or a story to increase brand awareness.

6. Instant Experiences on Facebook

Instant Experiences provide quick Facebook engagement on mobile platforms. These vertical ads load within 22 seconds and tell the whole message. These ad types suit perfectly when you want to obtain leads or gather contact data from your consumers. But there are many different things you can do with Instant Experiences.

•   Include relevant media to create a story-flow.

•   Use this type to highlight your product diversity.

•   Create interest in your business, so people decide to explore.

•   Give a clear pathway for viewers to reach your page or website.

•   Keep it responsive for mobiles.

• Add locations and site links to help viewers.

7. Story ads on Facebook

Stories are all over the Facebook platform after Instagram. These are images and videos that stay visible for 24 hours only. This popularity is used in ad campaigns with Automatic Placements. You can't specifically choose stories for ads, it is provided automatically, depending on your objectives. Selecting objectives such as video views, reach, app installs, traffic, brand awareness, and conversions help you leverage stories.

8. Messenger ads on Facebook

No marketer should forget Facebook Messenger when deciding an ad strategy. All kinds of ads get great exposure on messenger. You can tell brand stories, promote products and start a conversation with your target consumers.

Tips to Set Up A Great Facebook Ad In 2019

1. Make as many videos as possible

All formats of advertisement are blending in the video format. So, you can choose your creative and financial efforts on video ads to maximize the outcomes. No matter if you have products to sell, services to promote or want to create a personal brand, videos suit all objectives.

2. Invest 10% on community and brand building

As mentioned before, you need to find a balance of short-lived and a long-term marketing strategy. The long-term game should keep on running parallel with your other marketing campaigns. Use about 10% of the total Facebook ad budget to create ads that increase brand power and expand your community.

3. Monitor the ad frequency

High frequency of your ads will decrease the

results of your Facebook campaigns. The frequency of a Facebook ad shows how many times your target consumers see the ad. If the frequency crosses 2.5, it will start diminishing your returns.

4. Try different ad hooks

The hook is the ability of your ad to engage audiences and make them take the CTA. The hooks work only if they align with your audiences' interest, problems, needs, values, and convenience. An ad can offer to save money or time for an audience. Similarly, a different ad can offer a chance to resolve a problem.

You need to first evaluate your own business objectives. Then, find problems, which you can solve with those objectives. Choose market segments that face those problems and understand their emotions around that problem. Then, you can combine it all in your ad.

This approach will require various trials. You will get different kinds of results, but it is important to try various hooks to find the best approach and diversify your content quality.

5. Don't take too long to interact

Facebook Messenger ads, lead generation, and conversion-based objectives require an immediate response. These types of ads are business-focused and let you win contact and other information from your audiences. Messages allow your brand to begin a conversation on messenger with target consumers.

But it all should happen on an ongoing basis. You can't wait for the whole campaign to finish first and then reach out to interested consumers. Connect immediately after you receive the necessary response. This way, you won't have to put too much effort into the convincing process. The chances of purchase will increase on its own.

6. Decide a fresh ad budget every month

Business owners find it convenient to decide a

fixed ad budget for the Facebook platform. However, this is not a logical way of planning your ad budget. Seasons change, you get different levels of response rate in different zones, depending on what month of the year it is.

Keeping all that in mind, it is wise to define your ad budget every month. If there is a low period in your market, the sales and leads reduce. So, you should drop the ad budget during those months.

A great approach is to always ensure a high ROI with your ad campaigns.

7. Create a sense of scarcity

Apart from storytelling and human-based concepts, you should also include a sense of scarcity. This is really important when you want an immediate response from your target market.

Everybody wants to get an awesome deal. You can generate a sense that your products or services are available for a limited period of time. This works with offers, deals, discounts, and free packages as well. The potential buyers feel motivated to take action and purchase your product or service as quickly as possible.

8. Become a smart emoji user

When creating the copy of your ad, don't just revolve it around the text. Facebook is a platform where people express with emojis. So, you can use those emojis to enhance the convenience of consuming your ad copy. Even B2B ads can have emojis in them, as it is the current language of Facebook.

It is also important to know how many emojis are enough. You should use emojis to enhance a feeling and avoid overdoing it.

Now, you know all about Facebook ads. The objectives, the types and the methods of enhancing the quality of your ads. Though these are all directed towards Facebook, you can use the given tips on different social media platforms. These ad marketing tips will work on Instagram as well. You just need to use a creative approach with a little bit of common sense. That's all!

Chapter 7: Marketing With Instagram

Launched in the year 2010, Instagram has since shown a growth that was inevitable, as it was focused on the younger generation. Thanks to Facebook, this platform gained productive momentum. No other platform can sum up the phrase "a picture is worth a thousand words" better than Instagram. As of 2018, Instagram is believed to have 400 million active users. Initially, Instagram was started with the sole purpose of photo sharing, but it eventually evolved with various added features such as videos, stories, IGTV which means it has all features provided by YouTube.

Visual content is more appealing to the audiences and hence is one of the most popular forms of content online. Such content is shared most on the web and receives more engagement. Thus, it is considered as the most exciting platform.

The principal difference between Instagram and other social media networks is that it was only an App at first, which got the web site format recently. However, one can post videos and photos through the app.

People under 30, who consist of 59% of the platform strength and folks under 25 who spend an average of 32 minutes daily predominantly, use this media. 72% of teenagers use Instagram daily followed only behind Snap Chat. Instagram has recently got the story option, which is the same as Snapchat's artifact, which has helped Instagram's numbers elevate. Story option is exceptionally advantageous if your product aspires to win this generation.

If one aspires to spread his business internationally, then one must know that 80% of Instagram users are outside the United States of America. This is very useful if your offering can be ordered or used online, for example- A blog or a course. If one is based at a tourist destination, then this will have to be considered.

Instagram hovers around visuals or graphics. Hence, if your business depends on visuals, then this is the app for you. In addition, the feature of cross-sharing videos and photos to Facebook and Twitter is convenient.

Example, if you blog on cooking, then Instagram is a convenient mode to promote your articles. One can put up images of cuisine if you are planning to teach cooking from cookbooks and fresh content. A simple image can really attract a browser to a website or more details.

How to Use Instagram?

Profile making

The most valuable feature of your profile is your bio. Instagram allows 200 characters only, so you will have to put some time constructing a perfect one, as the characters may run out pretty quickly. Each word counts, so your bio must manifest what your company is.

Try to include the following information in your

bio:

Who are you?

What services are offered?

Why one must follow you?

Link to your business website or more information

Tips for A Great Bio

If your promoting business has a jingle or a slogan, Instagram is the place for it. A slogan aims at communicating the business idea and it can be placed in the bio section.

Include Emoji. Personality can be added to a bio and tone can be given, not necessarily a funny one, but the one that reflects your business. Example, if you're into photography, then include an emoji for a camera.

Include hashtags. Many corporates use marketable hashtags for campaigns on Instagram. By December 2018, Nike's #justdoit campaign has been tagged 16 million times. Just one hashtag is fine, avoid multiple. To avoid jamming up your bio and turn away followers keep all the tags at one place hence do not use too many hashtags.

Add specification to your header title. Header title is different from the username. Example, Samantha James, Scuba. It means that if someone searches for "scuba", her name will show up.

Provide your followers with some things "Extra". Like a coupon code or a link to a prized eBook, they will win if they enroll for your email. Provide them a taste of what you serve and what you provide if they purchase from you.

Things that could not be added to the bio can be added to your story.

Your profile picture must clearly disclose who you are and what you serve. Many use their logos, but there are other options. Ponder over a well-focused photograph that says it all about you.

Following And Followers

Being thoughtful of who you follow will impact your followers. The hashtags and accounts you decide to follow are the ones you impersonate. For example, you can follow the brands you appreciate.

Understanding brands that you follow provide a rich understanding of what works well and what doesn't. You can follow their engagement stats, on what generates more likes and comments, it helps you determine the brand's value and why people follow.

Furthermore, the activity of liking and commenting can bring traffic to your page as well. If you constantly browse pages and keep liking and commenting on them, the chances are high that people will check your pages as well due to your comments.

Posting Photos

Instagram revolves around the idea of posting pictures.

The best technique on what photo to post that will reflect your brand, is to think like a magazine editor.

In a magazine, editors carefully assess which photo or photos appear best, theme and the entire magazine. In short, the whole magazine is the selling point. Your photos should be akin to a magazine collage.

If you have a hard time with photos, then several apps will help you to present how the picture will look. Preview is one such free app, available on Google Play and Apple store.

One can try photo-editing apps. Several businesses use the same editing technique for all their photos, so they all look similar. Instagram offers editing techniques, but there are more to offer. Snapseed and VSCO are popular applications. VSCO is paid with a subscription fee of $ 20 per annum.

Most favorable time to post is between 12 pm to 1 pm from Mondays to Fridays. Instagram's algorithm is based on post engagement and not on chronological order. If possible, keep a set of draft posts this helps you post at your convenience, without the need to plan and then post.

Hashtags

Hashtags are signboards of Instagram. When Instagram folks search for an account, they usually get pushed to hashtags. Example if they search for food or sunset, it will lead to food or sunset images. Hence, if you just follow the hashtag, the post from the hashtags will be displayed on your feed. Hence, the judicious use of hashtag can generate more followers.

The type of hashtags you use will rely on the account type you are and the type of followers you want to acquire. If you want engagements then go for famous hashtags in the business that you are into but if you want long-term customers and followers, then get specific. For instance, if your target is a local business, then hashtag your city. Every post can use 30 hashtags and stories can use 10, use all and make sure it resonates your post.

Some Hashtag Tips

- Make a memo in any memo app so that you can simply copy and paste your post.

- Use your business hashtag so that your followers can use the same, for better results use them in captions.

- You can avoid making your post look too exaggerated with hashtags, although you have used all 30 tags, then you can simply comment on your hashtag.

- In case if you are running out of ideas, here are some example hashtags based on categories. Avoid simple copy and paste, as your hashtag must mimic your post or business.

Food: #foodie, #foodadda, #foodfood, #tastyfood, #yummyfood, #hungryforfood,

#foodonly, #foodorgasm, #foodallo

Travel: #travelog, #travelyahoo, #travelpore, #traveltravis, #explore, #unseenplaces

Fitness: #Moveit, #Fattofit, #gymed, #gymyboy, #fitman, #fitfreak

Stories

This feature was added recently to Instagram. Instagram stories were seen as an obvious copy to Snap Chat, which started it. Folks use it anywhere and a lot. Around 300 million stories are posted of which one out of five gets a direct message.

More so, they disappear after 24 hours, they are an awesome platform to endorse one-day offers and get attention to new material same way as Twitter does overfeeds.

Stories help add personality to your business or brand. From stories, one can disclose what your brand is. Also, you can add stickers, hashtags and links related to your business. One recent addition is the poll feature.

In this, you ask your followers questions and answer them directly, this is a very efficient way to approach your followers what exactly they expect from your business and even receive several engagements.

Ideas For Stories

- **Behind the scenes.** Are there some overwhelming or grand events that are necessary for your followers to view?

- **Promotion**. In case you have a one-day sale and you need to be vocal about it, stories are an amazing place for promoting due to their disappearing method.

- **Takeovers**. If you possess any influencer, who functions with your brand regularly, then allow them to overtake your stories for a few hours, it benefits both your brand and influencer.

Highlights

This feature allows you to organize the finest memories of your story into manageable reels. It offers you another platform for things you could not put in the bio.

Ideas For Highlights

- **Q & A highlights.** You have questions that are often asked by your followers on Instagram, and then FAQ highlight provides the space where you can compile all such questions.

- **Behind the scenes.** You have some illustrious images that add to the boldness and realness of your brand then put it here.

- **About us.** Details that you could not put in your bio, which you feel is essential like history, product manufacturing, customer views can be put in the highlight reel.

The most productive use of Instagram can be

made when the company is visual. Remember it's all in visuals.

Happy Instagramming!

Chapter 8: Marketing With Twitter

The seed for brands being on social media was first planted by Twitter. It enabled people to communicate with their favorite brand through its social media network, which gained popularity worldwide. Launched in 2006, Twitter has more than 336 million users globally.

The trend of communicating with the brands started through celebrities. Celebrities and politicians like Paris Hilton and Barack Obama discovered they could directly communicate with their followers on Twitter. On Twitter, any common person can tweet about the one they admire and get back a response. Basically, the grounds were even for all. Brands somehow realized it as a good business model to grow and adapted to the examples.

Nowadays, Twitter is considered as one of the best social media platforms to participate. Why?

The only reason is the common ground for all. Many brands involve themselves in constant communication with their customers. Brands like Denny's and Jet Airways tweet back to their customers, retweet their success stories and interact with them regarding their day to day lives. On Twitter, there is no broker between the customer and the source or you have to spend hours waiting on customer services; you just have to tweet regarding anything to reach the source. Many social media sites have implemented the same thing to their business page. For example, Facebook allows to post on a business's wall, but Twitter is the place to have a direct approach.

Twitter's userbase is very diverse. It has an equal number of men and women as active users, unlike other social media where the ratio is far from being 50/50. Millennials own the user catalog of Twitter. Almost 36% of Americans that are aged between 18 to 29-year-old use Twitter and approx. 80% of its userbase is millennials and 28% of people with college degrees and graduates use Twitter. Not only this the userbase of the Twitter base global, but around 79% of its user base is also not located in the USA.

Twitter uses photos, hashtags and numerals (stats or sports scores containing tweets) to encourage engagement. It thrives on things like these to engage people. Features like polling your followers add to the flavor. Brands use this as a method to reach out to people, tease their competitors and hence bring attention to both the brands and engage their followers.

What makes Twitter best is, it's real time and is very fast. The whole idea of Twitter is based on sharing what's happening in your life or around the world right now. On it, anyone can share quick updates about their life, new goal, projects or ask their followers questions. The character limit is just 260 characters per tweet, which is long enough to provide meaningful content and short enough to engage users.

So, the ultimate question is: Is Twitter right for

you? Yes, absolutely it is, Twitter can help any Business to grow, no matter it being a local brand or multimillion-dollar chain of brands. The only required thing is the customers or the clients you are planning to target is on Twitter and well, they probably are.

How to Use Twitter

Building your profile

Building a good Twitter profile is very important. It's very simple though. Once you finish up the bio section, which is the most difficult task in a profile, you are good to go. In a character limit of 160, you have to fit everything you want to tell about yourself. Your bio should be catchy and memorable. It should entice followers and explain everything you are. Don't worry about making it perfect in the first go, you will learn as you will get used to it.

Using effective keywords is the best approach to have a good bio. It need not be long sentences, it can be in a phrase of what you do. You could even mention the time of year you have been doing something. For example, "Selling newspapers since 2010". This means "newspaper" will be searched by people.

Using Slogans:

Create your own slogan. Good if you have already got one. Putting slogans into your bio can easily catch people's attention. Slogans represent the exact interest business is made on.

Being personal:

Personality forms the skeleton. Authenticity and transparency are always appreciated. Your followers are part of the community, so the most important thing to do is to make them feel like they follow you. For example, if you sell beauty products, something "Cheers to Beauty gurus!" leaves a tantalizing effect and makes your followers feel you are talking directly to them.

Use of humor:

Humor is used by a lot of businesses in their bio to gain the attention of their followers and entice people to observe their profile carefully. It's not very necessary to use humor but it has resulted in an increased number of followers. Sometimes using an inside joke which your people can only understand give you an edge and increase your followers.

Using hashtags:

Hashtags are used to categorize tweets and users. It makes your bio more engaging and specific. Using keywords of the category you want your bio to be in can give you an edge over other users.

Sending Tweets

Twitter works on a basic principle, the more you tweet the more followers you will have. The Twitter feed is very dynamic it changes every time because Twitter is all about what is happening now and "now" is always changing. In the highlights section of Twitter, the most engaged tweets are shown at the top, it instantly returns to that dynamic feed.

Due to this, even if your followers log in every

day, they still might not able to see your tweets. To make your tweets visible you have to tweet around 5 to 20 times a day, at proper time intervals. Since Twitter is global, 10 AM for you might be 5 PM for some of your followers.

Engaging with your follower is very important. Sometimes some brands just do advertisement and share links but not actually engage with their customers. This is not a good way to use Twitter. Engage with your followers, ask questions, reply to their queries and retweet often.

Say in present tweet what is happening right now. Following the trend, which could be easily found on Twitter, can boost your Twitter account. These things can be anything, for example, jokes, news or any stories. Tweeting about it using appropriate hashtags could put you in the limelight.

You should keep in mind a very important thing that Twitter regardless of its users asking to provide an edit option has not provided it yet. Be very careful while tweeting, proofread your content to avoid any unwanted debate or delete your tweet totally. However, if it happens, do not overreact, go with the flow and take responsibility for your error.

Retweeting

Retweeting is a way to share any tweet just like a share option on Facebook. You can retweet the tweets that you like or admire. The tweets can be of anyone you follow or your followers, brands you admire or anything that is similar or add light to your own brand. You can also retweet your tweet just to update your followers of something that you posted earlier or any progress on your previous tweet.

Following

Twitter allows people to see who you follow. This helps people to know what kind of people to follow or even just to get the idea of what kind of followers you want. Follow the people you wish to talk to in real life.

You should tweet a few times before you start following accounts on Twitter. Tweeting before following gives the idea of what your brand is all about and if interested they will follow you back.

Twitter Lists

Twitter lists are a very useful tool, but unfortunately, only a few make use of it. They are basically the list of people you follow organized categorically. Each category has a limit of 5000 people. You can create a list or follow any specific list you like.

Different ways you can categorize your list are as follows:

Geographically: You can create a list of businesses around your area if your business is located at one place like a store or a cafe. This list could be used to keep track of things happening locally.

Your industry: You should always keep yourself updated of people working in your industry or competitors, or anyone who has a business similar to yours. Keeping an eye on people in your industry would help you grow and also help you to make connections in your industry.

Pinned Tweets

Pinned tweets are tweets that are shown at the top of your profile. It depends on you when you want to change it. It can be changed every few weeks or every year.

Pinned tweets are about the things you are indulged with and are your top most priority. You can tweet about an event like a sale or hiring process and pin it at the top of your profile. This way if someone visits your profile, it will be the first thing they'll see.

Hashtags

As mentioned earlier, hashtags that are common in every social media were first introduced by Twitter. It was used to categorize tweets and Twitter users. Twitter has yet not announced a feature to follow hashtags like Instagram but it's probably coming.

Instagram allows 30 hashtags along with a caption; Twitter, on the other hand, demands to put hashtags in the same 260 characters limit. A business uses the hashtags that are trending and are relevant to their needs, to come into limelight.

Overall, Twitter is one of the most powerful platforms. It is fast and simple to use. It is necessary to use a social media site along with one or two. The most unique feature of Twitter is that it allows brands to directly engage with their customers. You can follow the most trending thing and be more aware of the surrounding than you already are.

Chapter 9: Marketing With YouTube

YouTube has gained popularity worldwide as the ultimate video sharing platform. YouTube was launched in 2005 and due to its popularity, Google bought it in the year 2006. It is one of the most popular websites in the world. YouTube ranks second in terms of monthly users after Facebook which is around 1.8 billion users every month worldwide. This number doesn't consist of people who don't have accounts and just prefer to watch videos rather than like, comment or subscribe channels.

Videos are the most engaging media format to be posted by people on social media. They are more likely to be liked, commented or shared among people. Videos gather attention within seconds by putting in very little efforts.

Even though YouTube is a social media platform but it doesn't really count as one because it acts more like a search engine, used to search videos of all types and hence ranks second after Google.

Unlike social media, YouTube contains all the videos posted on it and can be accessed by using keywords. It keeps a directory of all the media content ever posted on YouTube.

For example, someone posts a video of how to draw stick figures. Now if somebody searches "how to draw stick figures" in the search bar of Google or YouTube, all the relevant videos will be displayed no matter how old they are. The thing that decides the order of the videos is their engagement with the users and also the user's search history.

The YouTube algorithm is different from the rest of social media. The post made by people doesn't fade into the bottom of the feed after some time but is stored for eternity. The feed updates of YouTube is decided by the user's search history irrespective of the time it has been posted on social media. Therefore, it is the best place for marketing since you don't have to repeat the same post, again and again, to make it visible like twitter.

Marketing on YouTube is not an easy task. It needs some serious dedication to stand out in the crowd. Gathering subscribers are the most is a difficult task in YouTube marketing. You can post videos occasionally but every video needs to be properly written, well edited and streamlined. The content should be appropriate and good because of every minute approx. 400 hours of videos are uploaded on YouTube. Your content should be properly put together to stand out, so a proper knowledge of editing could be of great help.

Irrespective of all the hard work, YouTube is a great platform for any marketing campaign. It works well with the majority of other social networks and because of the search engine, you probably don't need to make new content (if having a lot of subscribers is not your goal). The best thing to do is to direct the crowd to your other pages.

YouTube is for everybody. It is a video platform, almost everybody watches videos of all types. Be it for entertainment purposes as well as for marketing. Anything you need is on the YouTube platform. It provides diversity in terms of users and content and that is why it becomes useful to make it a part of any marketing strategy.

YouTube videos can be made at a very low cost. It only needs a decent camera, be it your smartphone or you can borrow from a friend and that's it, you are good to go. It doesn't need industry standard equipment to make them. As long as you make sure it looks good, it doesn't matter how it's made. The quality of the content should be good, watchable, shareable without relevancy of the cost of creating it.

Mix YouTube with other social media sites like Facebook and Twitter, you can carry out a very powerful marketing campaign. YouTube alone can lead you to a dead end and make you feel restless. If you have websites, share your YouTube over them to obtain maximum results.

Starting Your Own Channel

Putting together a YouTube channel is very basic. This article gives a very good tutorial and with a little bit of curiosity hunt, you will be a master.

- **About Section**

The About section in YouTube is generally overlooked since it's hidden in the other tab when someone visits a YouTube profile. Whereas in other social media platforms, the About section or the bio is right in front of the profile visitor.

The character limit in contrast to the other social media is not limited but it still should be short and catchy. Think as if you just have 100 characters and make it as precise as possible, so that the most important thing goes into that section. Here, hashtags are not used.

At the end of the About section, add all the links

to your social media pages and websites. YouTube allows up to 5 links to be mentioned in the description, which is more than enough. You should also mention your business mail in order to entertain any possibility of collaboration.

- **Your Cover and Profile Image**

Profile image and cover photo should be simple and classy. Your logo can represent your profile picture very well and as for your cover image, a picture with your slogan would be perfect. Keeping it simple for starters is good. Just ensure that it is pleasing and catchy.

- **Your YouTube Trailer**

YouTube allows putting a video right in front and the center of your page. One thing that could be done is putting a trailer or a clip depicting everything your channel actually stands for. For starters, putting your best work up there could be the thing. The best video that you have got which best represents your company and your channel should be the first video your potential customers should see.

- **Making your Videos**

Ensure your videos to be unique and resonate with the theme of your brand. Make a list of video ideas, and separate the best ones. Watch videos of the same genre as yours and learn from them. Now when you pick up the camera, to actually make the video you should have an insight into how it should be.

It's not at all expensive to make a good YouTube video. The only things that are required is a decent camera, a tripod and good editing skills. Having a script is also a good idea, planning out everything what you want to say and how are you are going to do. Knowing exactly what you want from the video will help you make it better. The video should be very clear, the lighting should be the natural light if it is not available then create that type of lighting using some DIY techniques.

End the video with a call to action. Ending the video right away by saying goodbye is not a good way to end. Make sure you tell the viewers to subscribe, like and share your video among them. It will help you gain subscribers and market your brand and your channel. Asking them to comment below about how they feel about the video would help you to improve it next time. Encourage constructive criticism and try to know what they want in the next video. This is how the engagement of the viewers will be encouraged.

- **Titles, Description and Keywords**

Titles are very important on YouTube. As already mentioned, YouTube is more of a search engine than a social media platform and hence it works like that. The subject of your video should be properly stated in your title.

Descriptions are a great place to put the second most useful keywords. The priority of putting the best keywords should be in the title. The description should be precise and informative just like your About me section. Avoid spelling and grammatical mistakes. Such small mistakes make you look unprofessional.

The most important factor that is mostly overlooked by beginners on YouTube is the thumbnail of their videos. In the world of social media, the cover should say a lot and here the book is judged by its cover first unlike the real world. Make sure the thumbnail of the video is catchy, has the title in it, and is lit and focused.

- **Promotions**

YouTube can prove beneficial only when it's merged with other social media like Facebook and Twitter. To make YouTube a staple in your marketing campaign and prove it a success, you should share the details of your videos on other social networking platforms. You have to make sure your videos are shared among people. You have to let your followers know when your new video is being released with the help of other platforms.

But nowadays other social media platform are working to add video streaming platforms, for example, Instagram with IGTV and Facebook with their video content, it might prove less useful in this way.

Some Basic Tips

A lot of hard work and dedication is needed to make YouTube a success in your marketing campaign. Since YouTube needs entirely video content, it might take a considerable amount of time in contrast to other platforms. Remember this before deciding it to be your best fit.

- On weekdays, 12 PM to 4 PM is the best time to post videos, whereas on weekends it could be between 9 AM to 11 AM. Scheduling to post videos can be done on YouTube.

- Continuously promote your video on other social networking platforms. Tweet about it, release a trailer, a short clip in the stories. The more you promote the more successful the campaign would be.

- Before the promotion, at least have 5 to 10 videos already posted on your wall. This is done to keep the people attracted to you and made them believe that you know what you are doing.

- Consistency is very important. Fix a certain time to post your videos, like every Monday at 1 PM for example. The success of your channel depends a lot on your content and regularity.

- Choose content that you can make a video out of on a regular basis. If your video takes a month or two to build, it won't bring you success. A video a week is the minimum requirement.

- Promote your channel at the end of the video. Ask your viewers to like and subscribe to your channel. Engage them by requesting them to comment regarding the video or what they want next.

Types of Videos

•   **Tutorials**: To show how a product works or how it's set up. Show them how your services will affect their lives if your service is offering a service.

•   **Q & A:** Answer the question usually asked in your videos.

•   **Listicles**: Making videos for the "top ten". For example, "Top 10 gadgets of 2019" or "5 reasons why".

•   **Behind the Scenes**: This is a good way to humanize your brand. Show some inside story to connect with your viewers at a personal level. Show them you are all humans, you work hard and you all have fun. Show this to your followers to add a realistic touch.

•   **Vlogs**: making a video on how a day looks like working at your company. Talk to the camera and carry it around in a random manner, interview your employees in between. Make it as real as possible.

YouTube Analytics

Once you are done with a pleasing video, titles and keywords, it's time to move forward towards YouTube analytics. YouTube gives you the liberty to analyze all your videos posted on your channel. Which type of video is getting the most number of engagements, what kind of videos make users subscribe to, number of likes and other things. You can learn a lot about how to enhance your channel.

On YouTube analytics, you can analyze almost everything about your viewer's behavior, for example how long they stayed on your video. It also tells where people are watching your videos, from which device and from where they are finding them.

Using this information, you can enhance the user experience, enhance your channel and make your marketing campaign a success. Make the best use of this, and your YouTube channel will outshine everything.

Chapter 10: Marketing With Snapchat

Social media has grown so much, it is a lifeline for the youngsters. From the morning selfies to the food they eat, the places they go to and the things they do. Everything they like to post on social media.

Snapchat is one such social media application, which is available for both Android as well as iOS (Apple) platforms. The application works in a remarkably simple way through which people can send photos, texts, audio and video messages. However, the unique feature about Snapchat is after a certain time, the messages disappear. Around 47% of teenagers think that Snapchat is better than Facebook.

Initially, when the idea of Snapchat was proposed, people found it silly. Photos and messages disappearing after a certain amount of time seem so unrealistic. But today when we see the disappearing feature, it's the one which contributed to the success of Snapchat. Ironically, Snapchat's disappearing feature is one of the reasons for its success. However, it is not the only one.

The feature, which brought Snapchat to the list of most preferred and successful apps, is its story feature.

The basic idea of Snapchat revolves around the story feature. This application was created in order to make people more interactive and share their lives with others. If we summarize, Snapchat's main idea is to display what a person is doing in 24hours and in the form of Snapchat stories. Not all these stories can be seen after a period of 24 hours. This application proves to be a boon for all the businesspersons, in order to conduct 24hours contests and game plays.

Who do you think uses Snapchat the most? Among which age group is this application so popular? Obviously, the answer is youngsters. In case you have a product which has to be promoted among the youngsters, Snapchat is the choice for you.

Come off as unfiltered

Applications like Snapchat are aimed at the youth, as this is the only group who prefer to use such applications for fun as well as to be connected with their friends. Sharing each moment in snaps, making each snap fun filled is the main motto of Snapchat. Unlike other social media applications, Snapchat is all about fun because it is all about streaks of funny moments posted in stories. Some people love to share their day-to-day experience with others. They can easily do it by posting it on Snapchat as a streak of stories. The followers can see them and can stay connected to them. If you love to share your life and the happy moments with others, Snapchat gives you the perfect platform to do so and stay connected to your loved ones and your friends as well. Also, you can follow them and can see what interesting moments are they living their lives.

The main features of Snapchat are, when you take a selfie instead of keeping it plain and boring, you can add various filters to the selfies like puppy face. Draw and add emojis to make your photos more fun and interesting. As mentioned earlier Snapchat is all about fun, so all that fun should be reflected in your stories. The only age group which uses Snapchat are the youngsters, hence there is a great competition in the market. So make sure that your stories stand out of the crowd.

Posting

For making the pictures look goofy and funny, Snapchat provides a great range of such filters. Be creative is the sole motto of Snapchat. So add time, location, filters make them worth a see.

It can be confusing sometimes, what to post and what not to post out of so many pictures and filters which one to choose. Here are some suggestions in order to release that confusion from your mind:

- The more silly and funny your stories are, the more people prefer it. So share some behind the stage moments to make it look more creative and interesting. Get a tour of the backstage arena or the business place, and let your guide describe through the way.

- Consider account takeover: Record takeovers are fun, and they're commonly beneficial. What you do is you pick an influencer that reflects your image, and they assume control over your Snapchat feed for a specific measure of time, regardless of whether hours or days (this can additionally be finished with Instagram). This is an association that truly goes both ways: it brings regard for your image from the influencer's adherents, and it focuses on the influencer from your followers.

- Promotion Codes: The idea of Snapchat makes it perfect for notice of restricted time offers or occasions. It's going to vanish in 24 hours, and after it vanishes, it will never again be legitimate. If you're having a deal or an offer, that is an incredible spot to put it as just the general population who saw that story can really take the preferred standpoint of it.

- Put information just in your story that they can't go anyplace else exclusive. Certainties about up and coming undertakings, sharing data like this isn't just an incredible approach to make your adherents sense that they're on top of it and they're the first ones to know, it will likewise urge others to look out for you and tell you to make themselves feel like they're a section of that gathering. Your supporters are the best individuals on the planet, they merit that selective substance!

- Importance is your companion talk about current issues. Things that are occurring at the present time that can be anything from a senseless image that has turned out to be well known as of late or something that is enormously in the news currently. Talking about important issues demonstrates that you're truly in contact with the world. Just ensure that in some way or another, it relates back to your brand and that your supporters would really anticipate that you should talk about it.

- Occasion promotion: In the event that there is an occasion coming up, toss it up on Snapchat. When you're at the occasion, hand over the application to a few unique individuals so they can get the occasion from all diverse points into the story. Interesting points in the event that something is identified with your image in some way, snap it.

Seriously: See a statement? Meet somebody the organization works with? Have a photoshoot, Snap it. Your devotees ought to be there for each and every progression of the way. Try not to stress excessively over being great that it's not about the flawlessness factor.

Snapchat, since it's about what's going on in the minute. Nobody is impeccable in each and every minute, it's simply impractical. It's about these others' conscious minutes where every one of your breaks is uncovered and you're simply having a decent time. Your image will be increasingly relatable in the event that you post your entertaining and humiliating failings the same amount as you post your victories.

Keep them short, your snaps ought to be short clasps of your life, not an unscripted television appearance. You ought to give your supporters a cut, not the whole pie. In case you're going to stream an occasion, simply post scraps of what occurred. On the off chance that you truly need to post a whole video, post in Snapchat that there will be a Video posted on YouTube later, and simply post a little bit of it to your story. That way, your fans will go look at your YouTube page, creating more views for you. Ensure you share your Snapchat to your different pages by making a post about your Snapchat incidentally on your pages, and watch as individuals look to it.

Some of the time, a little push towards where you need them to go is actually what potential devotees need. Individuals may state that Snapchat is from the past, in any case, it's simply false. It is an immense platform, utilized by young individuals, and not exploiting that is senseless.

Happy Snapping!

Chapter 11: Marketing with Pinterest

Surely, the internet has revolutionized our lives. It has made its presence felt in each and every part of what one does in the world today, be it business, communication, information or entertainment. Even after the internet came, no one thought that it was ever possible to earn money through social media and other tools that the internet offers. However, with a lot of developments, it has been possible today. There are a lot of social media platforms that people use today as a part of their marketing strategies for the goods, services or personalities that they want to promote. Pinterest is one of those commonly used social media platforms which has a vast user base.

Pinterest has become an integral part of a marketing strategy in 2019, and the due credit goes to its popularity and reachability. There are a lot of saves and repins done on the Pinterest website or the app, however, the ultimate goal is to divert the traffic to one's own site. In order to help you achieve this goal, a few useful strategies have been listed below to facilitate Pinterest Marketing in 2019.

Leading Pinterest Marketing Strategies in 2019

- **Pin Punctually**

As a marketer, you know that this is a platform variedly used by the customers so you must be regular on it in order to make your presence felt. You must be using Pinterest consistently. Pinning once or twice a week will not be helpful to your agenda of driving traffic to your original site. If one finds manually pinning as laborious, then there are some Pinterest schedulers, which have a very smart strategy. They let you know of the smart time of creating a queue or pinning so that one does not have to pin manually. This is a clever strategy in helping to ensure your regularity.

Since the newer concepts are always evolving, there is an ad on to the basket, which questions if it is better to save directly from the website or repin a pin. This is a hack related to re-sharing your content on Pinterest. The answer to this is that it is better to save directly from the website with the help of the save tool. The must be sharing the seasonal content or the content which is always in use by pinning it directly from its website or blog post, etc. When this is done, the Pinterest scheduler makes sure that each pin is a new pin.

- **Create Several Pins Leading to the Same Source**

It is recommended that you create multiple pins which eventually lead to the same source. A different pin description is even recommended by Pinterest which helps in increasing the exposure in SEO and Pinterest Smart Feed. Therefore, you must consider creating different pins as well as different pin descriptions.

This hack is successful in getting you newer traffic from your old posts which might have already performed well. However, their reach can be increased this way. Your content, which might be evergreen or seasonal, gets better returns. You can try to create new pin images and apply them to your posts which are old. Along with this, your post can also be updated with new pins by using the "+" bar on the platform of Pinterest.

This is a clever way of reusing your old content and not let it go after it has been posted. This is useful also in the case if your post did not garner much traffic even though it was content driven, you could again give it a try by pinning it back with different pin images.

- **Contemplate Seasons Beforehand**

You must keep track of the important festivals, important days or holidays well in advance. Pinterest users usually start pinning ideas well before the actual occasion arrives. Therefore, your content must be in sync to that schedule and ready in advance. This helps you to drive more traffic to your content.

The users might pin the content or posts for Christmas maybe before one or two months or even before. Hence, it is recommended that you contemplate these seasons beforehand and develop your marketing strategy continuously ahead of the season.

- **Do Not leave Keywords on Boards**

This is a mistake which is done by a lot of people, that they leave the keywords on their boards. One must not forget that the board names are searched, even though less than the actual pins but it still does count. These keywords or board names help in making your SEO strong. You must assign some relatable keywords which might be searched in order to get to your content. Here, one must think like a user to be able to get to know this.

For instance, if your content is a recipe, then you can assign board names to it like, 'lunch recipe,' or 'egg recipe,' or even 'egg dishes.' Henceforth, if one searches something like this, then your content will appear for sure. Apart from this, you can also consider creating Sections on Pinterest if you think it is appropriate for your board as it plays an essential role in the search context.

- **Building a Follower Network**

In this marketing business, it is all about driving traffic to your spot. Therefore, the number of followers that you have plays a huge role in the process. It is not necessary for a person to be involved in the content creator's cause completely, it is about following the content creators that you love or you get inspired from or whose work is brilliant.

One must try to enhance its network of followers by engaging the people from your email list or your followers on other social media platforms to follow your content and your drive on Pinterest. Your Pinterest account can be simply boosted by asking your followers to get to connect to you on

Pinterest if that is already being done on some other platforms. You can engage them by sharing your profile with them. The reach of your content can be expanded exponentially by this strategy.

- **Use Hashtags**

Hashtags have started playing a hugely important role in the marketing strategies on social media platforms. They help your content trend. Therefore, you can write some specific and relevant hashtags in order to make it easier for people to find your work and get familiar with all that you have to offer to them. When one specifically talks of Pinterest, the hashtags there are treated as the search items. They are also associated with all the topics and issues which are trending and are being viewed by a large audience.

You can also see these hashtags beforehand and get to know all the topics which are trending so that you have something to contribute to it from your own side. Apart from these, you can also use the autocomplete suggestions by Pinterest, once you search your topic. This way, you can get to know about the hashtags which might work for your content, in case you are not able to decide the same.

- **Pay attention to your Descriptions**

If you simply post your content without describing it, then you are making it inconvenient for the audience which is going to judge your posts. The audience would not know what the post is about or what it wants to convey. Therefore, it is essential for one to provide a short description of the content that they are about to post. Strengthening the description also makes sure that it goes to the right kind of audience or the audience that you are specifically targeting. You must use full sentences in your description. This needs to be kept in mind while using keywords and the hashtags which are relevant to what your content is.

- **Persuade Saving on your Site**

If you want your followers or readers to be involved with you, then you must constantly persuade them or encourage them to save or pin on your site. This is useful in keeping them engaged with all that you have to offer to them. When you see people get involved with your work, you know that they can help you garner popularity by sharing your content with their network of people or persuade others to follow you as well.

- **Link your Instagram, Etsy and YouTube accounts with Pinterest**

This is an amazing hack which automatically increases your visibility once you link all your accounts with Pinterest. It increases your engagement when people from those platforms pin your content on Pinterest. Once you confirm these accounts with your Pinterest account, your reach is maximized. Along with this, it also helps to facilitate connection with your followers as they get to know you better after being connected on different platforms.

Customize Your Own Pinterest Marketing Strategy

There is no hard and fast rule that you have to follow these strategies rigidly and strictly in the way they have been defined. In case you do not wish to follow any of these strategies as they are, you can always introduce your touch to it by customizing it your way. There are a few things, which you need to consider before finally putting it into action. You can try to follow the steps listed below:

• **Define your aim:** The first step in this direction is to decide what you want to accomplish by getting your work on Pinterest. There are many things that can be achieved with the platform of Pinterest like, generating brand awareness, connecting with the influencers, increasing traffic to your blog or website, increasing sales or growing your database on email or all of them together. You need to define your boundary of aim that you would want to work for this cause and then devise a plan to go into a suitable direction.

• **Know your Target Audience:** In the world today, the market is run by the wants, needs, and capabilities of the audience. Therefore, before forming a product or service, it is always necessary to survey the needs and wants of the audience to which it has to go eventually. The audience determines the success or failure of a project. This helps you realize what they want and what they do not along with the problems they are facing and the potential solutions to those problems by your content. If you help the audience on Pinterest on the topics and issues they are concerned about, then there is a high chance of your success and popularity. This will be helpful for them in getting to know your work, your brand, and your beliefs. This gives you an opportunity to build trust with the audience.

You must also define your target audience in subcategories for a better formulation of strategies like you must see if it involves both men and women or what age group. This will help you figure out their potential interests and goals. This can help you in forming your content according to their tastes.

• **Decide the kind of images which will work for your business:** Since Pinterest is a platform which is hugely driven by pictures, you must be able to decide what kind of pictures would suit the business content that you are putting out there and expecting a response in return. Your pictures should be optimized according to the search engine of Pinterest along with them being according to the right size and type. The most important thing to be taken care of while devising a marketing strategy for Pinterest is the best quality pictures that go accordingly with the content which is being posted. Once you are found on Pinterest by the users, they can click on the pin and will come to your website.

You can lose the audience by providing them with poor quality pictures which might not be going with what you have put out there for them to see.

• **Focus on Management of your Pinterest Account:** When you are a business owner, you get to know that it is not possible to do all the things on your own and that you might need the help of some experts. If one tries to do everything on his own, then that will be a waste of time and energy and will lead to a lot of mistakes. Therefore, it might be better for you to give access to your Pinterest account to a person who is well aware of the know-hows of Pinterest Marketing. He must be aware of the ways he has to manage the account to bring that to your profit.

In case hiring a person specifically for this seems like a burden, then you can also start educating yourself on the same. There are a few online courses available for Pinterest Marketing that you can take, if interested. In case you do, you can look forward to being mentored by a person who knows all your concerns and will work all his might to teach you this.

• **Know your Competition and Learn:** When you are working in a business, you must know what and who your competitors are in the business. Being well aware of your competition contributes to your development as a whole. You must write down about your top two or three competitions and see what difference do they have in order for you to learn. You can see what the target audience loves about them, that maybe you can cover too and provide to them with your own twist.

• **Decide your Budget:** In order to keep your marketing consistent, you need to decide what and how many funds can you contribute to keep it going in the long run. Here, the key is consistency. You must keep the marketing strategy going. Therefore, it is significant to allocate funds for the same. You must have a budget, which allows you to hire a social media manager, bloggers, artists, or purchase or create good quality images. You can, therefore, set your limits accordingly and then evaluate if any section needs more funds or less in order to achieve your goal.

• **Get your Strategy Checked by an Expert**: It is good to apply all your will and hard work in formulating a strategy and deciding everything, but you need an expert to tell you what will work and what will not. You are going to need valuable feedback that will help you improve if nothing more.

If you consider all these steps, then for sure you will have a definite way to attract the audience.

It must have been helpful for you to know about all the popular and useful marketing strategies for Pinterest and how you can fulfill the goals that you decide. This helps in generating revenue, the thought which would have seemed abstract when the internet came. Since the internet came with its own pros and cons, it gave the opportunity to make most of all that it has to offer. Therefore, if you are doing this marketing strategy for a business, then you can expect rewarding returns in terms of the revenue.

Chapter 12: SEO Marketing

Marketing has its origin from the primitive period. In the barter system, the cavemen approached and tried to exchange the products he needed with his surplus products. As time passed, searching for the one who is in need of his surplus product became a tedious job. It consumed a lot of time and energy to get the products he needed in exchange for the products he produced in excess. Thus, marketing began as a way to sell goods and services.

Then there came the need to develop persuasive communications for selling goods and services. Marketing got further broken up into sales, marketing, advertising and retailing. This led to the concept of business development. The technological advancements in recent years have added further colors by shifting the concept of marketing to customer satisfaction, making it an indispensable part of the present day's business.

Today, digital marketing is the order of the day and an important concept that any online marketing professional has to understand is SEO marketing.

The Meaning Of SEO

SEO (Search Engine Optimization) is the process of organizing a website's content by topic, which helps search engines to understand a user's intent when searching for a particular product. It means gaining knowledge of how search engines work and using the experience to help a site perform well in search results, resulting in higher traffic and more leads.

The process of SEO starts with optimizing a web page around topics first, thereby ranking well for long-tail keywords related to that specific topic. It is a marketing discipline focused on growing the visibility of the website without any payment.

Simply put, the use of SEO practices for online marketing of any product, service, or company is known as SEO Marketing. It encompasses technical and creative elements that will be required to improve rankings, drive traffic and increase awareness in search engines that will result in more leads and revenue generation to the company. It improves visibility and brings the traffic thereby constituting a powerful marketing tool.

Its purpose:

When a person enters a query on a search engine, there appears a list of various information and websites relevant to the query. SEO Marketing filters the query by relevant content and matches it with the respective topic that contributes to lead generation and conversions in a business.

Various things contribute to SEO Marketing. Amongst that, the principal reason would be the audience. Analyzing the needs and behavioral pattern of the target audience is the key to marketing which SEO provides with the simplest of efforts. The second reason is the emerging trends. Information technology has boomed to a large extent. Now, people are able to find out from search engines using voice search. These keep changing and marketing is also to be updated to the current trend. Next in the line is algorithmic changes.

Search engines like Google deploy web crawlers, which crawl on every website and collect all the information on it and match it with the algorithm specified by Google and the results that fit the specified criteria are displayed on top, not to leave out technological advancements. With the advent of machine learning, SEO is rapidly changing. The intent is an important signal and the SEO community must adapt and help Google connect audiences with the right content at the right time to deliver the best content experience. Technology is changing every day and will continue to shape every aspect of how we practice SEO.

Benefits Of SEO Marketing

- **Organic way of promoting**

businesses – SEO Marketing is the best way of promoting business in an organic way. The dominance of the business can be established without any payment.

- **Increased visibility** - SEO Marketing Companies makes use of algorithms and optimizes the ranking of different online portals and businesses. This results in a large inflow of traffic to your website that naturally leads to the generation of more leads and better chances of their conversion.

- **Cost-effective:** When SEO is implemented, you can reap the benefits with no need to spend on marketing. Therefore, this has become one of the most cost-effective methods of optimizing the online presence of any business. Further, the results due to SEO optimization are long-lasting and help in enjoying great returns.

- **Changing algorithms:** The algorithm of the search engines are an ever-changing aspect on which SEO results are dependent on. Because of this, we can consider that the SEO actions as complementary to the mechanisms of search engines.

Factors That Contribute To SEO Marketing

The ranking in the search engines depends on so many factors that will ensure the business a better online presence. These are:

- **Domain Authority** – Relevance of the domain name with the content it presents are an important factor that is a measurement of trust that your website has gained based upon some factors like age and backlinks. This is commonly known as Domain Authority. Also, domain names which are shorter are favored by search engines more than the long domain ones.

- **Keywords** – These are an important

factor for SEO Marketing. The use of right keywords with keyword tools such as Google keyword planners or those that can be gathered during a brainstorm session should be made use of. Based on the keyword strategy, low, medium or high competition keywords or a mixture of two that will appear in the heading or subtitle of the contents can be used as an input for SEO.

• **Relevancy** – Search engines have evolved to be smarter than most people. They can find out easily if the result is an original or plagiarized-one. Hence, it is always better to hire efficient workers who will help develop the business in an original way. In other words, you can expect to get higher points on SEO when you have relevant links on your website.

• **Links** – Inbound links are more favored by search engines. If the links are from a reputed and relevant source, then you can even get additional brownie points.

• **Content-Length** – Content-Length is a

major factor influencing SEO. If website articles or blogs are of greater length, they rank higher. So, for writing a blog post, it is better to write a detailed description of the subject.

• **Loading Speed of the Site** – Search engines like Google prefer a site that loads up quickly. Hence, for an SEO optimized website, one has to take care of the loading time.

• **Design Compatibility** – Today, most people are more comfortable with searching from their mobile. Therefore, while optimizing a website, one has to keep in mind the compatibility with all types of devices. This ensures you have a clean, responsive and functional website.

• **URL Structure** – Search engines favor URLs, which are uncomplicated and easy to understand along with being descriptive as well as to the point. Short URLs are better, but there should be no compromise on including important keywords in the URL to have good SEO

Marketing.

Sometimes, due to over-aggressive or shady SEO tactics, it is possible that SEO could go horribly wrong. These may be due to Algorithmic Penalties, Cleanup Up Link Related Problems and many others. However, the Google Search Console comes to your rescue at that time. It will help you patch up what has gone wrong and recover the business to the original position. So, sufficient care has to be taken while implementing SEO and the experts must be aware of how it can impact the business reputation. The main focus of SEO should be brand building and the common mistakes have to be avoided.

The impacts of SEO Marketing:

Once the SEO has been successfully implemented, we need to know its impact on the business. There are various ways by which the value addition of SEO can be analyzed. One of the ways would be through measuring Organic Sessions. These sessions measure earned visits to your website from search engines such as Google and Bing, the actions taken by the user during that visit, and also the exit of the user from the site. If a user is inactive for more than 30 minutes, the session becomes idle by default.

You can integrate the data with a reporting tool such as Agency Analytics or Google Analytics to better cross-reference with other data points. Another method could be by analyzing the increase in Keyword Ranking – It is always better than the frequently searched keywords on your website contribute to the high volume keywords ranking index. Various tools such as SEMRush or SE Ranking can be used to track keyword rankings in a website. One more important method in this context is the Leads to Conversion Ratio, which means the generation of a lead that is most probably likely to convert into a sale. This ratio accounts for the major success of SEO. An increase in the number of leads means more business to you.

Therefore, if tools like Google Analytics and rank

tracking, the heat map is combined with SEO practices to amplify strengths and correct weaknesses on your website, it is a successful SEO Marketing.

Conclusion

Things to Keep In Mind

Note that you can learn a lot from this book. Every time you read it, you may feel overwhelmed with the knowledge this book deals with. In this chapter, here the things you should keep in mind and how all of that works.

What are the most important things to keep in mind?

- **Transparency:** There should be transparency between the promoters and the customers. Sharing "behind the scenes" moments can make a major impact on the customers. They can enjoy the wow moments of your life as well. This basically helps in making the brand more popular and humanizing it.

- **Authenticity:** The most important part of any business is being yourself. Being yourself makes your business different from others. This is the best way to gain the trusts of the customers as they believe in originality. So, never pretend to be someone else and make your own way instead of following others' paths.

- **Variety:** Bringing variety in your products enhances your business. Sticking to the same old product will bore the customers, which eventually will bring the customer rate down. Use the same formula with a little variation every time as it helps to increase and promote the product in a much effective way.

- **Current events**: Being up to date for any business is really important because no one prefers an outdated version. Updated products give tougher competition in the market. Gather information about what is happening in the world and modernize your products according to that.

- **Visualization:** People say that the first

impression is the last impression, therefore, make your first impression worth a watch. Make your profile colorful and attractive by using interesting patterns and colors to make it look prettier and handy. A simple but creative interface is what people want nowadays.

- **Have a plan:** Proceeding without a plan can sometimes prove to be fatal. It's always better to design a plan first before starting any work.

- **Know your brand:** Exaggeration is possible if you don't know much about your brand.

- **Engage:** Keeping your customers engaged is one of the main parts of any business. It's because of them, the business is reaching its heights. Never ignore a customer review or their problems about the product.

- **Mistakes make us learn:** Mistakes are steps towards success, therefore, never give up on any mistake. Learn from the mistake and continue the work with the same spirit. Don't let failures overcome you.

- **Avoid social media mistake**: Be careful while posting anything on social media as even a single mistake can be noticed by people. Before posting anything, get a thumbs up and then only proceed with it.

- **To not have at least an idea of what you're getting into:** Before getting yourself into the work, have a clear and proper idea about what you know about the product or the brand. Also, be clear into your mind about the goals and the motto of the brand and the product. Don't get yourself into any unnecessary trouble.

- **To understand your goals:**

Understanding the goals of any brand is very important. Without knowing the exact cause and the goal you cannot promote the brand. It won't give justice to the product. So understanding the goal is really important.

- **Not having high expectations:** Having hopes is fine, but high hopes can lead to disappointment. For anything to get popular, it takes time and efforts. If you are expecting an overnight jump in your popularity or views on the post, you are expecting too much. Social media is a place where you have to promote your brand as well as gain the trust of the people in order to make it more popular.

- **Humanizing your customers**: Without the customers, a business cannot rise as they are not just for squeezing out money for your business. So, listening to their comments and views about the product is the first priority.

- **Thinking before you post:** Be smart before posting anything on social media. Check it twice, take advice from an expert then only post anything. One mistake can lead to great damage to the reputation of the product. Therefore, don't let your hard work go in vain just because of a single mistake.

- **Not being tone deaf:** Make sure your posts stick to the events. The trends you are sharing on social media should be the latest and public approved.

- **Don't share too much:** Ever heard of TMI? Sharing too much can also bring problems sometimes. Only the required portions of any information shall be shared. Spilling too much private information can prove to be fatal at times.

- **Stick your opinions to your**

business: There are thousands of things happening around you, but giving your opinion on every one of them is not important. Social media is one such platform, which provokes people to share their opinions on any unnecessary topics as well. Thus, it's advisable to stick your opinions just to yourself and your business. Sharing of the point of views related to business can be advantageous.

Mistakes can happen anytime by anyone, but the important part is how you deal with them and rectify them so that they don't happen again.

Social media is not that bad as it sounds, it is fun at times, though. The basic criteria are how much do you want to get involved in your life. As per a business point of view, learning customer problems and views can be fun. In addition, social media provides that fun until you use it for a positive purpose. Promote the positives of your business and enhance your business.

Final Words:

Thank you so much for your time to choose this book for learning about social media marketing. While a lot of the things that you need to do in this marketing strategy is the same as what most marketers have been following, yet a few changes have also been seen. It is because of such changes that you can bring your brand up in the market and beat your competition. Do follow the information provided to you in this book to get the best benefits out of it.